Welsh Heritage
Food & Cooking

Welsh Heritage
Food & Cooking

Best-loved national dishes shown in 65 step-by-step recipes
and over 240 stunning photographs

Annette Yates

Photography by Craig Robertson

LORENZ BOOKS

This edition is published by Lorenz Books

Lorenz Books is an imprint of Anness Publishing Ltd
Hermes House, 88–89 Blackfriars Road, London SE1 8HA
tel. 020 7401 2077; fax 020 7633 9499
www.lorenzbooks.com; www.annesspublishing.com

If you like the images in this book and would like to investigate using them for publishing, promotions or advertising, please visit our website www.practicalpictures.com for more information.

© Anness Publishing Ltd 2006, 2007

UK agent: The Manning Partnership Ltd, 6 The Old Dairy, Melcombe Road, Bath BA2 3LR; tel. 01225 478444;
fax 01225 478440; sales@manning-partnership.co.uk

UK distributor: Grantham Book Services Ltd, Isaac Newton Way, Alma Park Industrial Estate, Grantham,
Lincs NG31 9SD; tel. 01476 541080; fax 01476 541061; orders@gbs.tbs-ltd.co.uk

North American agent/distributor: National Book Network, 4501 Forbes Boulevard, Suite 200, Lanham, MD 20706;
tel. 301 459 3366; fax 301 429 5746; www.nbnbooks.com

Australian agent/distributor: Pan Macmillan Australia, Level 18, St Martins Tower, 31 Market St, Sydney, NSW 2000;
tel. 1300 135 113; fax 1300 135 103; customer.service@macmillan.com.au

New Zealand agent/distributor: David Bateman Ltd, 30 Tarndale Grove, Off Bush Road, Albany, Auckland;
tel. (09) 415 7664; fax (09) 415 8892

A CIP catalogue record for this book is available from the British Library.

Publisher: Joanna Lorenz
Senior Managing Editor: Conor Kilgallon
Project Editor: Emma Clegg
Designer: Nigel Partridge
Illustrator: Robert Highton

Photography: Craig Robertson
Food Stylist: Fergal Connolly
Home Economy Assistant: Sophia Winfield
Prop Stylist: Helen Trent
Production Controller: Claire Rae

3 5 7 9 10 8 6 4 2

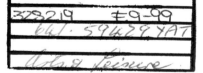
NOTES

Bracketed terms are intended for American readers.

For all recipes, quantities are given in both metric and imperial measures and, where appropriate, in standard cups and spoons. Follow one set, but not a mixture, because they are not interchangeable.

Standard spoon and cup measures are level.
1 tsp = 5ml, 1 tbsp = 15ml,
1 cup = 250ml/8fl oz.

Australian standard tablespoons are 20ml. Australian readers should use 3 tsp in place of 1 tbsp for measuring small quantities of gelatine, flour, salt, etc.

American pints are 16fl oz/2 cups. American readers should use 20fl oz/2.5 cups in place of 1 pint when measuring liquids.

Electric oven temperatures in this book are for conventional ovens. When using a fan oven, the temperature will probably need to be reduced by about 10–20°C/20–40°F. Since

ovens vary, you should check with your manufacturer's instruction book for guidance.

The nutritional analysis given for each recipe is calculated per portion (i.e. serving or item), unless otherwise stated. If the recipe gives a range, such as Serves 4–6, then the nutritional analysis will be for the smaller portion size, i.e. 6 servings. Measurements for sodium do not include salt added to taste.

Medium (US large) eggs are used unless otherwise stated.

CONTENTS

Wales: a culinary introduction

Wales has a strong tradition of living off the land that stretches back as far as the ancient Celts. It is a tradition that was to survive well into the 20th century in parts of rural Wales. The fare was simple but wholesome and was designed to satisfy the hearty appetites of hard-working farm labourers, coal miners, quarry workers and fishermen.

Surprisingly little is documented about cooking in early Wales. Probably the best- known cookery book (and the only one in English) was *The First Principles of Good Cookery* by the Right Hon. Lady .

Below *The Wye Valley and the Vale of Usk, from the northern Black Mountains to the rural valleys around Newport, are areas of outstanding natural beauty.*

Llanover, Lady Augusta Hall. While it made little impression at the time, it is now valued as a fascinating insight into life in a large house on the south-east border of Wales. Lady Llanover was also influential in improving Welsh culture – including sponsoring and entering competitions at the Eisteddfod, encouraging Welsh speaking, and obliging her staff, tenants and guests to wear traditional Welsh rural clothes.

Generally, however, traditional culinary skills were passed on from Welsh mothers to their daughters as they worked together in the kitchen. In fact so little had been written down that the culinary heritage of Wales was in danger of being lost completely after women began working in jobs outside the home.

That is, until Minwel Tibbott, a staff member at the Welsh Folk Museum (now the Museum of Welsh Life) began voice-recording the memories of old people all over Wales during the early 1970s to the 1990s. At this time, the people of Wales seemed unaware (and often denied the fact) that they had culinary traditions, even though they often recalled the "old foods" with enthusiasm and nostalgia. In homes and restaurants, cooks and chefs were eager to shake off the thrifty dishes made with just a few simple ingredients in favour of more elaborate dishes valued by the English. Maybe the Welsh had simply eaten them far too often in the past? Perhaps those traditional dishes, made with such limited ingredients as were available at the time, proved too uncomfortable a reminder of days when Wales experienced much poverty. Or perhaps the Welsh people simply needed to move on after the recent World Wars, when women discovered roles outside the home. Nevertheless, the everyday dishes of Wales are delicious. They are a valuable part of the heritage of Wales, one that is certainly worth preserving.

Today Wales has embraced its culinary heritage and is now justifiably proud of its food culture. It enjoys world recognition for much of its produce and Welsh chefs are acknowledged among the best in the world. Welcome to Wales, or *Croeso i Gymru!*

Geography of Wales

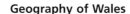

Wales, the peninsula that projects from the western side of Britain, covers an area of about 20,000 square kilometres (7,700 square miles). At its widest point it measures 200 kilometres (124 miles) east to west and 250 kilometres (155 miles) north to south. The region is a mass of mountains deeply dissected by rivers. There are three national parks and five areas of outstanding natural beauty, which together cover a quarter of the

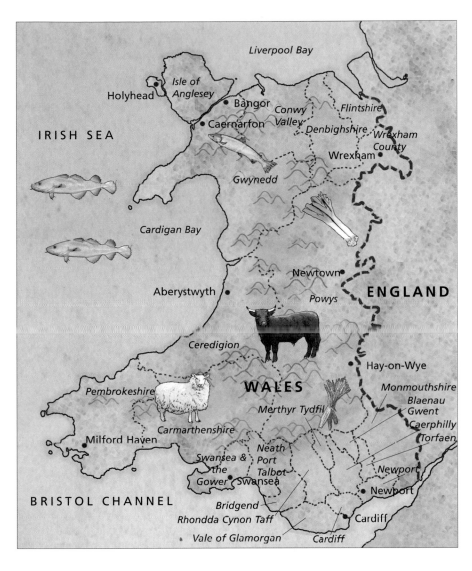

came the booming wool trade and all efforts were switched to rearing sheep. Ever since, Wales has been known for the vast numbers of sheep to be found on its mountains and in its valleys, at home both in mountainous terrain and the damp lowland climate. Today the uplands have cattle too, often the Welsh Black, also at home in lush lowland pastures (see Hafod and hendre on page 11).

In common with most hilly regions in Britain, oats and barley have long been staple crops grown in the rural uplands, where the climate is cold and wet. By the end of the 19th century, oats had become of considerable value to every farmer and oatmeal was one of the basic ingredients in the family's diet. The lowlands, with their fertile valleys and rivers, provide conditions more suited to growing wheat and vegetable crops. It is also where the dairy herds thrive best.

Wales has a coastline that has been a rich source of fish and other seafood, with Milford Haven formerly having one of the largest fishing fleets in the UK. The coastal marshlands are also home to a speciality of the region, saltmarsh lamb.

Below A shepherd and his dogs moving a flock of sheep up the hills to graze on summer pastures.

Above *Surrounded by the sea on three sides, the peninsula of Wales is a mass of mountains divided by rivers.*

area of Wales. There are craggy peaks, peaceful valleys, picturesque lakes and reservoirs galore.

The mountains have been a rich source of minerals, yielding slate in the north, and coal and iron ore in the south, as well as lead, copper, silver and gold. The varied landscape with its strong contrasts influences the food of the region and 80 per cent of the land is dedicated to agriculture, from livestock to crops.

The rural uplands were once dominated by goats and cattle. Then

A culinary timeline

Well into the 1900s the foods of Wales were mostly sourced locally from mountains, lowlands, rivers and sea. Meanwhile culinary traditions derived from the working classes, unlike in England where they came down from the upper classes. This timeline provides a brief insight into the development, survival and revival of the traditional foods and dishes of Wales.

10th century The Romans brought herbs, vines and the daffodil to Wales. The Welsh *Laws of Hywel Dda* (Hywel the Good) mention the only two vegetables cultivated in Wales – leeks and cabbages. With so few vegetables available, meat was central to the diet. When meat (usually bacon) was supplemented with some vegetables and cooked in a large pot over an open fire, it formed the basis of the traditional broth or soup called "cawl".

12th century Giraldus Cambrensis (Gerald the Welshman), writer and cleric, wrote of a rural Wales with flocks, milk, cheese, butter and oats. It was on these staple foods that the Welsh subsisted well into the 19th century.

16th century Watermills were introduced for processing oats, rye, barley and, later, wheat. Food was

Below These huts provided some shelter for the laver gatherers at Freshwater West, Pembrokeshire, c.1930.

Above An 18th-century water mill located by the River Teifi at Cenarth, in south-west Wales.

cooked over open fires, directly over which cast-iron kettles, cauldrons and bakestones were placed for boiling, cooking and baking, and above which bacon was smoked and cured.

17th century Rural life still dominated Wales and people were largely self-sufficient – with the exception of sugar, salt, tea, rice and currants, which had to be bought in. Wall ovens, either built in (stone or fire-brick) or portable (clay) ones, began to appear close to the English borders in south-east Wales.

18th century Rural Wales was made up largely of tenant farmers and gamekeepers, and hunting was a popular sport among the upper classes.

Mid-18th to mid-19th century With the industrial revolution, people moved from rural Wales to the coal-mining valleys, the iron and steel works of the south, and the slate quarries of the north. Previously the Welsh had been mostly self-sufficient (even the smallest cottage would have had a small plot of land on which to grow food). Now they were forced to buy their foodstuffs. In addition, diets were influenced by those of immigrants (including English, Irish, Italians, Polish and Russians), who also flocked to the areas in search of work. In this period that was renowned for

poverty, and the importance of meat and vegetables was reversed, with cawl now made with extra leeks, cabbage, potatoes and root vegetables and very little meat.

19th century The increasing need to transport goods produced during the industrial revolution resulted in improved road and rail communication, at the same time bringing in a greater variety of non-native foodstuffs and refined foods – commercial flour, cheap sugar and chemical raising agents. By mid-century only about one third of families in Wales were supported by agriculture, and the country became the world's second industrial nation (England was the first).

Small wall ovens became a common feature in large farmhouses, though they proved inadequate for baking bread in anything but small quantities. So home-prepared bread dough was taken to communal ovens for baking.

In 1896, the Report of the Royal Commission on Land in Wales described the conditions and circumstances under which land was held, occupied and

Above *A cattle auction at Newport cattle market with an attentive collection of local farmers.*

cultivated. It mentioned home-cured meat (mainly bacon), home-grown vegetables (mostly leeks, carrots, cabbages, herbs and potatoes), dairy products (milk, butter, cheese) and cereal-based dishes.

20th century Cardiff became the largest exporter of coal in the world. Home cooking still reigned, with home-cured meat, home-grown vegetables, dairy products, oats and barley as mainstays. Daily and weekly meals continued to follow a strict pattern – breakfast, main midday meal, tea and supper. Open chimneys with wall ovens were gradually being replaced by enclosed ranges.

After World War II the restaurant trade began to emerge but it mostly ignored the culinary heritage of Wales, instead looking to England and further afield for inspiration. The attempts were not successful and resulted in a poor reputation.

In homes, gas and electricity were introduced and old-style dishes started to be discouraged (new recipes for new cookers) and people moved away from the monotony of cawl and stews. By the late 1900s the "old" dishes were perhaps unwelcome reminders of less affluent times though they were eaten on special occasions and promoted to tourists in particular. All the while, Wales continued to produce its excellent-quality meat, dairy foods, vegetables, fish and shellfish.

The final decades of the 20th century saw Wales at the forefront of organic farming (particularly in Ceredigion) and beginning commercial production of its own foods and drinks.

21st century Wales now takes pride in supplying some of the finest produce, with emphasis always on freshness, quality and variety. It enjoys international recognition for its beef and lamb, and its fresh fish and seafood, as well as its unique cheeses. There is an increasing number of skilled and innovative chefs in Wales, eager to make full use of local foods supplied by artisan food producers. There are Welsh food awards called *Taste of Wales* and many restaurants, hotels and guest houses are featured in the best-known food guides. There are farm shops, farmers markets and food festivals.

Cardiff, Wales' capital city, is a cosmopolitan district with a range of ethnic foods available in its markets, shops and restaurants. Development is ongoing in the bay area of Cardiff, where the new National Assembly building (the *Senedd*) and the Wales Millennium Centre (the country's premier arts centre) are situated. To conclude, Wales is without question a vibrant place to live and work.

Below *Late summer harvest time in the Dyfi Valley, Powys, located in the heart of rural Wales.*

Customs & traditions

Wales has a wealth of customs and traditions, some of which are described here in brief. More detailed information can be found in the Museum of Welsh Life at St. Fagans, near Cardiff.

The Welsh language

Wales has always had Welsh-speaking strongholds even when the language has been in danger of dwindling during the last 20 years. Over this time a campaign for Welsh heritage has helped ensure the survival of the language, and today an enthusiastic revival has seen the number of Welsh speakers continuing to rise.

Folklore

Myths, legends and folklore are plentiful. In addition to the set of medieval Welsh tales called *Mabinogi*, the names of Merlin the mythical magician and King Arthur, legendary ruler of Camelot, still live on in compelling tales and place names all over Wales.

Welsh gold

Mined in north Wales, Welsh gold has been especially valued for making jewellery for centuries and dates back to the days of the Celtic kingdoms, when aristocrats wore gold armbands (torcs) to signify their authority. Echoing that ancient tradition, the British royal family wear wedding rings of Welsh gold.

Music and poetry

Two things intrinsic to Welsh life are music and poetry – they are found in the chapels, in competing choirs, at rugby matches and in the National Eisteddfod, one of Europe's largest and oldest cultural festivals (dating back to the 12th century). Strongly linked to the eisteddfod is the Gorsedd of Bards, a group of poets, writers, musicians and artists who have made a distinguished contribution to

Welsh language, literature, and culture. And let's not forget poets Dylan Thomas and R.S. Thomas, opera singers Geraint Evans and Bryn Terfel, and popular singers Shirley Bassey and Tom Jones.

Rugby

The nation's favourite sport since the 1800s, rugby started as a middle-class game but soon became very popular with the working class of the industrial south, who would turn up at matches with home-cooked pies and pasties. Today, the Welsh are as passionate as ever about rugby, and support international matches wearing leeks, daffodils and the Welsh flag.

Lovespoons

The tradition of giving a lovespoon as a romantic token dates back many centuries. The carving of a lovespoon from a single piece of wood on a cold winter's night was a popular pastime and intricate symbols were used to relay particular meanings. These days, lovespoons are popular souvenirs of Wales and are given as gifts for all sorts of occasions.

Above *A tempting selection of sea food on display at the Cardiff Indoor Market in South Wales.*

St David's Day

On 1 March Wales celebrates its patron saint, *Dewi Sant*, with concerts, choir performances and other special events. Primary school children dress up in Welsh costume and it is traditional to wear a daffodil or a leek, both considered to be national emblems, and have Welsh names that are similar. In the past, Welsh armies were known to wear leeks to distinguish them from their foes; today leeks are more likely to be seen at international rugby matches. St David's Day also sees the Welsh flag bearing the red dragon hoisted all over Wales, and mealtimes centring on traditional dishes, such as cawl and roast lamb.

Markets, drovers and country fairs

The weekly market, or mart, was important for selling livestock and food in the 18th and 19th centuries, with one in every town and several fairs during the year providing the excuse for a holiday and feasting. Drovers would walk animals

Above *Welsh black cattle in Gwynedd, Snowdonia. The beef from this breed receives international acclaim.*

(often 200 cattle or 1,000 sheep) from the local market to centres in England. With the coming of the railways, transport and ways of selling changed, and markets and fairs changed or petered out. Today, locally produced food is sold in town markets, including Swansea, Cardiff and Carmarthen. There are also regional markets, the increasingly popular farmers' markets and annual county shows, the largest of which is the Royal Welsh Show held near Builth Wells.

Hafod and hendre

To ensure ample food for his animals throughout the year, the Welsh farmer developed the custom of dividing the year between two homes. At the end of autumn he would move his animals to the lowlands to shelter over winter and he would live in the *hendre* (or old habitation) in the valley. In spring he would move his animals to the mountains to graze while he moved to the *hafod* (his summer dwelling), leaving the valley free to grow crops

during summer. This custom has long ceased, but *hafod* and *hendre* remain as farm and village names all over Wales.

Hospitality

A visitor knocking on the door of a traditional Welsh household could always be sure of a warm welcome. After being fussed over and with some bustling in the kitchen, visitors would not be allowed to leave without having a bite to eat – some quickly made pancakes or Welsh cakes to be eaten hot off the bakestone. It has always been a tradition in Wales to offer food as gifts – to celebrate weddings, childbirth and New Year's Day as well as to support friends and neighbours in times of illness or bereavement.

Welsh dresser

Together with the hearth, the Welsh dresser was originally the focal point of the kitchen, a place for cooking and eating as well as the warm room where the family spent most of its time and where visitors were welcomed. The dresser would be stacked with plates, cups, saucers, jugs and dishes.

Baking day

It was customary, once a week, for every household to have a marathon baking day, when a huge quantity of baked goods would be prepared for the week ahead. Bread, bara brith, cakes and Welsh cakes were popular choices for the traditional Welsh tea (alas no longer indulged in on a regular basis) and for the packed lunches known as "boxes". The tradition is still kept up (though on a smaller scale) in some homes today.

Meal times

After a traditional breakfast of bacon, eggs, laverbread and cockles, the main meal was eaten at midday. Welsh tea was the late afternoon ritual, with home-baked bread, butter, cheese and jam, and maybe bara brith or Welsh cakes. Supper, at around 8–9pm, was not considered a meal but a seasonal, light-but-savoury snack, maybe fish or wild mushrooms. Sundays and special occasions warranted roast meat and rice pudding.

Below *A Welsh dresser, dating from around 1880, loaded with gleaming plates and dishes.*

***Above** A kettle hangs over the kitchen grate. Welsh housewives were skilled at cooking and baking on an open fire.*

Herbs in cooking and in healing

The main cooking herbs were savory, thyme, mint and, more recently, marjoram and rosemary. Long before they were used for cooking, herbs were well used for healing the sick. This art was especially important in the 13th century with the physicians of Myddfai, a family of physicians who lived in Carmarthenshire. It is believed that their descendants continued to practice until the 18th century.

Cawl

Meaning broth or soup, cawl was once an integral part of life in Wales – a broth, a stew and a soup containing all the goodness of the land in one pot and eaten daily. It started simply with home-cured bacon, leeks, cabbage, potatoes and water. When these basic but flavourful ingredients were left to simmer gently in an iron pot over a fire, or on a range, for hours – even days – the fat skimmed off for frying and baking, they turned into something that still provokes nostalgia in the older generation of the Welsh. And no cawl was ever the same, for its contents would vary with the region, the season and the cook. It was originally served in wooden bowls and eaten with wooden spoons. So comforting was the dish that when the weather is cold, people are still heard to say "It's cawl weather".

Cawl has been served as a one-pot meal for several generations now, though originally the broth would have been served separately from the meat and vegetables.

Cooking on the open hearth

Since prehistoric times, food has been cooked in cauldrons or cooking pots over an open fire. Complemented with the bakestone or griddle, this continued throughout the 18th and 19th centuries and, in many places in Wales, well into the 20th century. Such limited facilities determined what could be cooked. Stews, joints and puddings were boiled in the cooking pot supported on a tripod with hook and chain. There were spits for roasting and, for small roasts and baking bread, the iron pot would be inverted over a bakestone to form a makeshift oven or pot oven, with glowing embers piled on top of the inverted pot. Later came the Dutch oven, a three-sided box that was hooked on to the grate with its open front facing the fire.

The bakestone

Only in Wales has such extensive use been made of the bakestone or griddle. Using it has required great skill and ingenuity by the cook. The original bakestone was a flat stone (later it was constructed from iron or slate) that was placed over an open fire or on the hob of a range. A slender wooden spade or slice was used for turning cakes, breads, pancakes, scones, oatcakes and pastry turnovers and pies. The bakestone was used extensively until the turn of the 20th century when built-in wall ovens appeared in farmhouses. Even then, the oven would be heated one day a week, with the bakestone used on other days.

Modern bakestones are designed to suit modern appliances. The traditional iron bakestone is suitable for use on the solid plates of ranges, on gas hobs and on electric hobs with solid plates. The new anodised aluminium alloy bakestones are lightweight and suit all hobs, except the induction type.

An old, well-used bakestone is likely to need little greasing during cooking. A new bakestone may need regular greasing to prevent food from sticking, particularly when cooking foods containing sugar. The handles of a heavy bakestone get extremely hot, so thick oven gloves are a must. You will also need to make sure you have somewhere safe to leave it to cool.

The bakestone must be heated to an even, all-over temperature for cooking. The heavy, traditional style needs time to achieve this, so put it on to heat while you prepare the ingredients. The temperature of the bakestone surface will depend on the food being cooked. Let experience be your guide, holding your hand just above the surface to judge progress, and check the temperature by testing a small amount of food first.

***Below** Modern bakestones are light and easy to use; they heat evenly, need little greasing and are simple to clean.*

Native foods

Here is a brief introduction to the key ingredients that have been traditionally grown and cultivated in Wales.

Cereals

Until the early 20th century, oats played a fundamental role in the Welsh diet. Oatmeal was made into semi-liquid dishes, many of which involved long, skilled and arduous methods – flummery (from the Welsh word *llymru*), sowans (or *sucan*), thin flummery (called *bwdram*), porridge (*uwd*) and oatmeal gruel (*grywcl ceirch*). Oats and barley were made into bread, wafer-thin circular loaves cooked on a bakestone. In north Wales, oat bread was made into pottages – shot (*picws mali* or *siot*) and brose (*broes*).

Vegetables

Originally, leeks and cabbages were the two vegetables cultivated in Wales. Later came root vegetables, such as swedes and carrots, with potatoes available from the 18th century. Pembrokeshire is known for its new potatoes. A wide variety of vegetables are now grown – particularly in Pembrokeshire, the Gower Peninsular, the Vale of Glamorgan and the Usk Valley.

Below Tyn Grug *(left) from Ceredigion and* Teifi *(right) from Carmarthenshire are both unpasteurized, organic cheeses.*

Fruit

Wales has never produced much fruit as the soil and climate is not suitable. Fruit trees – apples, plums, damsons and medlars – were planted first on a semi-wild basis and then in gardens and yards, along with gooseberry bushes and a rhubarb patch. These days, soft fruits grow successfully in the mild climate of the Vale of Glamorgan; in south-east Wales apple growers make delicious apple juice. Cider is produced on the mid-Wales borders, and the south-facing slopes of Monmouthshire and the Vale of Glamorgan are home to several vineyards. Dried fruit, a mainstay of Welsh baking, was brought to Wales by the Normans.

Milk, cream, butter and buttermilk

Milk has always been a popular drink and is widely used in cooking (salmon is cooked in milk and milk is an essential baking ingredient). Cream, too, is used in sauces, and records show it being used in desserts from the 1600s. The Welsh

Above Ever since the 1st century, cabbage, together with the leek, has remained central to Welsh cooking.

have always had a particular fondness for butter – traditionally they liked it salty and enjoyed it thickly spread on bread and melted in copious quantities over pancakes. Buttermilk has been used as a drink and in baking.

Cheese

Cheese-making has a long tradition in low-lying areas of Wales. Until the 1600s, goat's and sheep's milk was used followed by cow's milk. Once the fat from cow's milk had been removed to make butter, the resulting skimmed milk was made into cheese, which on its own was unremarkable both in texture and flavour.

Below Most gardens boasted a gooseberry bush or two.

However, the Welsh found the ideal way to deal with it and toasted or "roasted" thick slices of cheese (*caws pobi*) in front of an open fire before serving it on toasted bread. This was the foundation of Welsh Rarebit and it remains a firm favourite.

The cheese industry suffered difficult times in the early 1900s but it has since flourished to produce the wonderful range of cheeses available today. Caerphilly is probably the best-known traditional cheese of Wales – this brined cheese was originally made in the principality. Today there are several producers, including the award-winning Gorwydd Caerphilly from Ceredigion. There are other award-winning cheeses too, such as Llanboidy, Llangloffan and Nantybwla, all of which are hard-pressed varieties made with unpasteurised milk. There are also cheese-makers supplying artisan products at local farmers' markets, from mature farmhouse Cheddar styles to washed-rind and blue-veined cheeses, soft goat's cheeses and creamy buffalo cheeses.

Fish

Wales has always enjoyed a plentiful supply of sea- and freshwater fish, although recent years have seen much of it sold direct to other countries. Along the west coast of Wales herring and mackerel prove the most popular catches, while hake started the speciality fishery in Milford Haven. Travelling fish vans were a common sight all over Wales until the mid-1900s. Today diminished supplies may include bass, brill, monkfish, plaice, skate, sole and turbot.

The fast-flowing rivers of Wales have always provided grayling, wild brown trout, salmon and sewin, though here stocks are also dwindling. Until recently, traditional methods of catching river fish survived. The "coracle", first created in prehistoric times, was once a familiar sight on the Teifi, Tywi and Taf. This is a small lightweight circular vessel that has changed little over the years. Its basket-weave wooden frame would have been covered in hide and waterproofed with tallow, later to be replaced with calico or canvas and sealed with pitch and tar or

bitumen. Two coracles, with a net strung between them, would drift down river with the current and pick up salmon and sewin.

Wales's coastline has also been a good source of shellfish – including cockles, crabs, limpets, lobsters, mussels, prawns, razor fish, scallops and winkles. Oysters were once plentiful on the Gower Peninsular, though now supplies are sparse and they have become an expensive luxury. The cockle industry on the Gower Peninsular still thrives and for hundreds of years, cocklemen and women have raked up the little heart shapes along the sands of Penclawdd. Swansea market has a range of stalls dedicated simply to cockles and to another traditional Welsh delicacy, laverbread.

Above *Brill, from the turbot family, is a small flatfish with soft, white flesh.*

Laverbread

Often referred to as "Welshman's caviar", laverbread (*bara lawr*) is a seaweed (laver) boiled to make a soft dark green mass. It is an acquired taste and is a traditional part of a full Welsh breakfast, heated as it is or mixed with oatmeal and cooked in fat as little cakes.

Meat

Before the 18th century, only leeks, cabbage and root vegetables were grown. Ever since then meat has played a vital role in the diet of the Welsh.

Though Wales is probably best known for its lamb, the mainstay has always been the pig, with the pig sty

Below *Dried laver, made from the seaweed used for the Welsh delicacy laverbread.*

(*twlc* in Welsh) at the bottom of the garden a common sight in rural areas and some built-up areas of the mining valleys. Pig-sticking (as the day the butcher came to slaughter the pigs was known) brought great excitement and a dish of hot faggots, made that same day with the fresh innards, to celebrate the occasion. There would also be sausages, brawn and puddings to be made, steaks to be fried, ribs to be roasted, fat to be rendered and bacon to be cured.

Young Welsh mountain lamb enjoys international recognition today. In days gone by, however, cooks would not have tasted the meat from lamb. Instead, they enjoyed the more interesting texture and flavour of mutton, and even that was considered a rare treat to be reserved for high days and holidays. Today, mutton is making a welcome comeback. Both mutton and saltmarsh lamb from Wales are now considered to be great delicacies.

Welsh black beef, meanwhile, enjoys a similar profile to Welsh lamb. Wales' native cattle breed dates back over 1,000 years and is equally at home in craggy uplands or lush lowland pastures. Before the days of banking, Welsh black cattle were often used as currency, when they were dubbed "the black gold from the Welsh hills", and led to the development of one of the first banks – the Bank of the Black Ox. The breed was even depicted on the banknotes.

Poultry and game

Poultry has always been important in Wales, with many households keeping a few hens, ducks and geese in the yard. Their eggs were cooked for the family or sold to raise a small income. Though older hens have always been used for stews, right up until the mid-1900s roast birds were reserved for a treat or for special occasions, such as Michaelmas, Christmas or New Year. The feathers from geese were used in the home – for bedding, for dusting and sweeping, and in the kitchen for brushing up oatmeal or flour during baking. Naturally reared venison now comes from large estates. In several areas of Wales there are organized shoots for wild duck, partridge, pheasants, woodcock, snipe and hare.

Wild foods

The Welsh countryside is rich with wild pickings. There are blackberries in the hedgerows, orange rowan berries on the mountain ash trees, blue-black sloes on the blackthorn branches, and purple whinberries or blueberries on the low bushes on the hillsides and moorlands. In the autumn there are hazelnuts and wild mushrooms in the woodlands, in fields and on coastal cliffs. Elder flowers can be collected in early summer or elder berries in the autumn. Wild sorrel grows on the river banks, ideal for sauces to serve with fish. Wild garlic grows in abundance in the woodlands. Its young leaves can be added to salads or used as a wrapping for whole fish, such as trout, while its lacy white flowers look pretty in salads. Salt marshes all around the coastline of Wales are home to marsh samphire and sea beet, both lovely served with saltmarsh lamb.

Above Cockles are raked up on the sands of the Gower Peninsula.

Rock samphire can sometimes be found on the coastal cliffs of the south. Then there are cockles, mussels, winkles and, occasionally, crabs and rock prawns.

Honey, mead and spices

In Wales, as in the rest of Britain, honey was the first sweetener and is still used in cakes and to flavour lamb. Mead, made by fermenting honey, water and yeast with herbs, spices or flowers, was the earliest alcoholic drink and is currently experiencing a revival. Ever since the Middle Ages the Welsh have loved to use spices in their cooking, with ginger being a particular favourite.

Sea salt

Harvesting the natural sea salt from the Atlantic waters around the island of Anglesey is one of Wales's recent success stories. The snowy white crystals of Anglesey sea salt, with their crunchy texture and clean flavour, are now highly prized.

Left Whinberries grow on low bushes on the Welsh hillsides, often alongside heather.

Appetizers, light meals & breakfasts

Anyone visiting a Welsh household is likely to be offered traditional appetizers and light meals. Maybe a steaming bowl of cawl (a hearty soup) made with leeks and potatoes and flavoured with home-cured bacon, or a savoury dish in which cheese, eggs or leeks star as the main ingredients. To begin the day, the traditional full breakfast is usually accompanied by the Welsh delicacy laverbread, served on the side or mixed with oatmeal and cooked in hot bacon fat.

Leek soup

This is an adaptation of the traditional method, where a piece of bacon flavours the *Cawl cennin*. Two generations ago, bacon, vegetables and water were put into the pot early in the morning and left to simmer over the fire all day. It often made two courses or even two meals – the bacon and vegetables for one and the cawl or broth for the other.

Serves 4–6

1 unsmoked bacon joint, such as corner or collar, weighing about 1kg/2¼lb

500g/1lb 2oz/4½ cups leeks, thoroughly washed

1 large carrot, peeled and finely chopped

1 large main-crop potato, peeled and sliced

15ml/1 tbsp fine or medium oatmeal

handful of fresh parsley

salt and ground black pepper

1 Trim the bacon of any excess fat, put into a large pan and pour over enough cold water to cover it. Bring to the boil, then discard the water. Add 1.5 litres/ 2¾ pints fresh cold water, bring to the boil again, then cover and simmer gently for 30 minutes.

2 Meanwhile, thickly slice the white and pale green parts of the leeks, reserving the dark green leaves.

Cook's tip
For a quicker version fry 4 finely chopped bacon rashers in butter before adding the vegetables in step 3, and use chicken or vegetable stock in place of water.

3 Add the sliced leek to the pan together with the carrot, potato and oatmeal. Then bring the mixture back to the boil, and cover and simmer gently for a further 30–40 minutes until the vegetables and bacon are tender.

4 Slice the reserved dark green leeks very thinly and finely chop the parsley.

5 Lift the bacon out of the pan and either slice it and serve separately or cut it into bitesize chunks and return it to the pan.

6 Adjust the seasoning to taste, adding pepper, but please note it may not be necessary to add salt). Then bring the soup just to the boil once more. Finally, add the sliced dark green leeks along with the parsley and simmer very gently for about 5 minutes before serving the leek soup.

Per portion Energy 273kcal/1135kJ; Protein 18.8g; Carbohydrate 10.9g, of which sugars 3.5g; Fat 17.3g, of which saturates 6.3g; Cholesterol 53mg; Calcium 33mg; Fibre 2.7g; Sodium 1550mg

Spiced parsnip and apple soup

Hardy root vegetables, including parsnips, grow well in Wales. Their sweetness marries well with a sharp apple juice, such as that made from the single variety apples (some rare) grown at Gellirhyd Farm, near Crickhowell. A small amount of curry paste or powder spices up the flavours of this soup, called *Cawl pannas ac afalau.*

Serves 4-6

25g/1oz/2 tbsp butter

1 onion, finely chopped

1 garlic clove, finely chopped

500g/1lb 2oz parsnips, peeled and thinly sliced

5ml/1 tsp curry paste or powder

300ml/½ pint/1¼ cups sharp apple juice

600ml/1 pint/2½ cups vegetable stock

300ml/½ pint/1¼ cups milk

salt and ground black pepper

natural (plain) yogurt and chopped fresh herbs, such as mint or parsley, to serve

1 Melt the butter in a large pan and then add the onion, garlic and parsnips. Cook gently, without browning, for about 10 minutes, stirring often.

2 Add the curry paste or powder and cook, stirring, for 1 minute.

3 Add the apple juice and stock, bring to the boil, cover and simmer gently for about 20 minutes, until the vegetables are very soft.

4 Purée the soup with a blender or in a food processor and then return it to the pan.

5 Add the milk and seasoning to taste.

6 Reheat the soup gently, stirring, and serve topped with a spoonful of yogurt along with a sprinkling of herbs.

Cook's tip
To make it more chunky in texture, purée just half the soup in step 4.

Variation
Replace the parsnips with a winter squash, such as butternut.

Per portion Energy 130kcal/548kJ; Protein 3.4g; Carbohydrate 18.5g, of which sugars 12.6g; Fat 5.3g, of which saturates 2.9g; Cholesterol 12mg; Calcium 101mg; Fibre 4g; Sodium 56mg

Anglesey eggs

This delicious dish of potatoes, leeks, eggs and cheese sauce, *Wyau Ynys Môn*, is traditional to Anglesey. A nice variation is to add a little freshly grated nutmeg to the cheese sauce. Instead of browning the dish in the oven, you may prefer to finish it by putting it under a medium-hot grill.

4 Pour the milk into a pan and add the butter and flour. Stirring continuously with a whisk, bring slowly to the boil and bubble gently for 2 minutes, until thickened and smooth. Remove from the heat, stir in half the cheese and season to taste.

Serves 4

500g/1lb 2oz potatoes, peeled

3 leeks, sliced

6 eggs

600ml/1 pint/2½ cups milk

50g/2oz/3 tbsp butter, cut into small pieces

50g/2oz/½ cup plain (all-purpose) flour

100g/3½oz/1 cup Caerphilly cheese, grated

salt and ground black pepper

1 Cook the potatoes in boiling, lightly salted water for about 15 minutes or until soft. Meanwhile, cook the leeks in a little water for about 10 minutes until soft. Hard-boil the eggs, drain and put under cold running water to cool them.

2 Preheat the oven to 200°C/400°F/ Gas 6. Drain and mash the potatoes.

3 Drain the leeks and stir into the potatoes with a little black pepper to taste. Remove the shells from the eggs and cut in half or into quarters lengthways.

5 Arrange the eggs in four shallow ovenproof dishes (or use one large one). Spoon the potato and leek mixture around the edge of the dishes. Pour the cheese sauce over and top with the remaining cheese.

6 Put into the hot oven and cook for about 15–20 minutes, until bubbling and golden brown.

Cook's tip
The leeks could just as easily be cooked in the microwave in a covered dish: there is no need to add water. Stir once or twice during cooking.

Per portion Energy 540kcal/2259kJ; Protein 26.6g; Carbohydrate 41.3g, of which sugars 12.3g; Fat 30.6g, of which saturates 16.2g; Cholesterol 345mg; Calcium 471mg; Fibre 5g; Sodium 443mg

Salad of Carmarthen ham with smoked salmon

This famous dry-cured Carmarthen ham is Wales' answer to Italian prosciutto, French Bayonne and Spanish Serrano or Iberico hams. Its flavour is rich and deep and a little can go a long way. In this salad, *Salad cynnes ham Caerfyrddin gydag eog mwg*, it is paired with hot-smoked salmon, served in a warm dressing of olive oil, lemon juice and spring onion.

Serves 4

90ml/6 tbsp olive oil

100g/3½oz Carmarthen ham slices, cut into wide strips

4 spring onions (scallions), thinly sliced

300g/10½oz hot-smoked salmon, skin removed and roughly flaked

30ml/2 tbsp lemon juice

mixed salad leaves, such as spinach, watercress, frisée, little gem and lollo rosso

1 Heat the oil in a pan. Toss in the ham and cook quickly until crisp and tinged with golden brown. Lift the ham out on to a plate

2 Add the spring onions and salmon to the hot pan and sprinkle in the lemon juice. Once warm, return the ham to the pan. Arrange the salad leaves on plates and spoon the ham and salmon over.

Per portion Energy 288kcal/1196kJ; Protein 24.1g; Carbohydrate 1g, of which sugars 1g; Fat 20.9g, of which saturates 3.3g; Cholesterol 41mg; Calcium 27mg; Fibre 0.4g; Sodium 1712mg

Cheese pudding

Old recipes for this classic dish, *Pwdin caws wedi pobi,* involved cooking layers of toasted bread and cheese in the custard mixture. This version, which uses fresh breadcrumbs, is light and soufflé-like. Serve it with green vegetables, such as beans or broccoli, or with a crisp salad tossed in an oil and vinegar dressing.

Serves 4

225g/8oz/2 cups grated mature Cheddar-style cheese – Llanboidy or Llangloffan are particularly good

115g/4oz/2 cups fresh breadcrumbs

600ml/1 pint/2½ cups milk

40g/1½oz/3 tbsp butter

3 eggs, beaten

5ml/1 tsp mustard (such as English or wholegrain) or 2.5ml/½ tsp mustard powder

salt and ground black pepper

1 Start by preheating the oven to 200°C/400°F/Gas 6. Then carefully butter the insides of a 1.2 litre/2 pint/ 5 cups ovenproof soufflé dish.

2 Mix together three-quarters of the cheese with the breadcrumbs.

3 Put the remaining ingredients into a pan and stir well. Heat gently, stirring, until the butter has just melted (if the mixture gets too hot then the eggs will start to set).

4 Stir the warm liquid into the cheese mixture and tip into the prepared dish. Scatter the remaining cheese evenly over the top.

5 Put into the hot oven and cook for about 30 minutes or until golden brown and just set (a knife inserted in the centre should come out clean).

Variations
Stir a small handful of chopped fresh parsley into the mixture before cooking, or put a layer of soft-cooked leeks in the bottom of the dish.

Per portion Energy 534kcal/2232kJ; Protein 27.5g; Carbohydrate 29.5g, of which sugars 7.9g; Fat 33.9g, of which saturates 20.2g; Cholesterol 227mg; Calcium 656mg; Fibre 0.6g; Sodium 803mg

Welsh rarebit

The Welsh have always loved "roasted" cheese. In its simplest form Welsh Rarebit, *Caws wedi pobi*, would traditionally have consisted of a slice of bread and a large slice of hard cheese, each toasted in front of the open fire. Just before the cheese had a chance to soften too much, it was laid on top of the crisp bread and served.

Serves 2

2 thick slices bread

soft butter, for spreading

10ml/2 tsp ready-made mustard of your choice

100g/3¾oz Cheddar-style cheese such as Llanboidy, or crumbly cheese such as Caerphilly, sliced

ground black pepper

pinch of paprika or cayenne pepper

tomato wedges and basil leaves, to garnish (optional)

1 Put the bread on the rack of a grill (broiler) pan and put the pan under a hot grill both sides are lightly toasted.

2 Spread one side of each slice of toast with butter and then a little mustard (or to taste). Top with cheese slices.

3 Put under the hot grill until the cheese is soft and bubbling and beginning to turn golden brown.

4 Sprinkle with a little black pepper and paprika or cayenne and serve immediately, garnished with tomato wedges and basil leaves (if using).

Variation
As an alternative method, use a mixture of cheeses, grated and stirred together with the butter and mustard before spreading them on the toast and grilling (broiling).

Per portion Energy 386kcal/1611kJ; Protein 18.4g; Carbohydrate 25.8g, of which sugars 1.4g; Fat 23.7g, of which saturates 13.5g; Cholesterol 59mg; Calcium 442mg; Fibre 0.8g; Sodium 652mg

Leek, goat's cheese and hazelnut tart

Wonderful goat's cheeses are made in Wales today, from soft cheese and soft-rind logs to hard varieties that are ideal for cooking. If your cheese is particularly strong you may want to use the smaller quantity listed in the ingredients. This tart, *Tarten cennin, caws gafr a chnau barfog* is best served hot or at room temperature.

Serves 6

85g/3oz/¾ cup hazelnuts, skinned

175g/6oz/1½ cups plain (all-purpose) flour

115g/4oz/½ cup butter, chilled and cut into small cubes

15ml/1 tbsp olive oil

350g/12oz/3 cups leeks, thinly sliced

5 eggs, lightly beaten

425ml/¾ pint single (light) cream

2.5ml/1½ tbsp wholegrain mustard

175–225g/6–8oz/1½–2 cups hard goat's cheese, such as Merlin, grated

salt and ground black pepper

1 Toast the hazelnuts in a dry frying pan, in a hot oven or under the grill (broiler), until golden. Leave to cool, roughly chop half and finely chop the rest.

2 Sift the flour and seasoning into a large bowl and stir in the finely chopped nuts. Add the butter. Using your fingertips, rub the butter into the flour until the mixture resembles fine breadcrumbs. Sprinkle over about 45ml/3 tbsp cold water, mix until the crumbs begin to stick together and then gather the mixture into a ball.

3 Roll out the pastry and line a 25cm/10in flan tin (pan). Put in the refrigerator for 10–25 minutes to rest (or leave it there until required).

4 Put a baking sheet in the oven and preheat to 200°C/400°F/Gas 6.

5 Put the oil and leeks into a pan and cook until soft, stirring occasionally. (Alternatively, place in a microwave-proof dish, cover and microwave on full power for about 5 minutes, stirring once).

Variation
This is equally good made with crumbled Caerphilly cheese: use the larger quantity listed in the ingredients.

6 Prick the base of the pastry case and line with baking parchment and dried beans. Put on to the hot baking sheet and cook for 10 minutes. Remove the paper and beans and brush the pastry with beaten egg. Return to the oven for 3–4 minutes.

7 Meanwhile, mix together the remaining eggs with the cream, mustard, half the cheese and a little seasoning. Stir the mixture into the leeks and pour into the hot pastry case. Sprinkle the rest of the cheese on top and scatter the remaining (roughly chopped) hazelnuts over the top or around the edges.

8 Put into the hot oven and cook for about 30 minutes until set and golden.

Per portion Energy 683kcal/2835kJ; Protein 20.7g; Carbohydrate 26.9g, of which sugars 4g; Fat 55g, of which saturates 27.3g; Cholesterol 267mg; Calcium 381mg; Fibre 3.1g; Sodium 409mg

Leek, bacon and egg pie

In this dish, *Pastai cennin, bacwn ac wyau,* leeks (the national emblem of Wales) are used to make a sauce that is teamed with bacon and eggs to make a delicious family meal. Here the pie is topped off with puff pastry, although shortcrust pastry would be just as good. Serve it with freshly cooked seasonal vegetables or a mixed salad.

Serves 4-6

15ml/1 tbsp olive oil

200g/7oz lean back bacon rashers (strips), trimmed of rinds and cut into thin strips

250g/9oz/2 cups leeks, thinly sliced

40g/1½oz/⅓ cup plain (all-purpose) flour

1.5ml/¼ tsp freshly grated nutmeg

425ml/¾ pint/scant 2 cups milk, plus extra for brushing

4 eggs

1 sheet ready-rolled puff pastry

salt and ground black pepper

1 Preheat the oven to 200°C/400°F/ Gas 6. Put the oil and bacon in a pan and cook for 5 minutes, stirring occasionally, until the bacon is golden brown.

2 Add the leeks to the bacon. Stir, cover and cook over medium heat for 5 minutes until slightly softened, stirring once or twice.

3 Stir in the flour and nutmeg. Remove from the heat and gradually stir in the milk. Return the pan to the heat and cook, stirring, until the sauce thickens and boils. Season lightly with salt and pepper.

4 Tip the mixture into a shallow ovenproof pie dish, measuring about 25cm/10in in diameter. Using the back of a spoon, make four wells in the sauce and break an egg into each one.

5 Brush the edges of the dish with milk. Lay the pastry over the dish. Trim off the excess pastry and use it to make the trimmings. Brush the backs with milk and stick them on the top of the pie.

6 Brush the pastry with milk and make a small central slit to allow steam to escape. Put into the oven and cook for about 40 minutes until the pastry is puffed up and golden brown, and the eggs have set.

Per portion Energy 202kcal/842kJ; Protein 13.4g; Carbohydrate 9.7g, of which sugars 4.4g; Fat 12.5g, of which saturates 4.2g; Cholesterol 149mg; Calcium 125mg; Fibre 1.1g; Sodium 592mg

Glamorgan sausages

When is a sausage not a sausage? When it is a Glamorgan sausage! These meat-free concoctions were made at least as far back as the 1850s. George Borrow recorded his appreciation of them during his travels in Wales, when *Selsig Morgannwg* were served for breakfast. They are delicious served with a crisp salad and a fruit-based sauce or chutney.

Makes 8

150g/5½oz/3 cups fresh breadcrumbs, plus extra for coating

100g/3½oz/1 cup mature (sharp) Caerphilly cheese, grated

1 small leek, washed and thinly sliced

15–30ml/1–2 tbsp chopped fresh herbs, such as parsley, thyme and a very little sage

5ml/1 tsp mustard powder

2 eggs

milk to mix, if necessary

plain (all-purpose) flour, for coating

oil, for deep-frying

salt and ground black pepper

1 In a large mixing bowl, stir together the breadcrumbs, cheese, leek, herbs, mustard and seasoning. Separate 1 egg and lightly beat the yolk with the whole egg (reserving the white). Stir the beaten eggs into the breadcrumb mixture. You need to add sufficient milk to make a mixture that can then be gathered together into a sticky (although not wet) ball.

2 Using your hands, divide the mixture into eight and shape into sausages of equal size. Cover and refrigerate for about 1 hour, or until needed.

Cook's tip
They won't be quite as crispy, but you can fry the sausages in shallow oil in a frying pan, turning them occasionally, until golden brown on all sides.

3 Lightly whisk the reserved egg white. Coat each sausage in flour, egg white and then in fresh breadcrumbs.

4 Heat some oil in a deep fat fryer or large pan to 180°C/350°F. Lower the sausages into the oil and cook for 5 minutes until crisp and golden brown. Lift out, drain on kitchen paper and serve immediately.

Per portion Energy 202kcal/844kJ; Protein 7.6g; Carbohydrate 17.6g, of which sugars 1g; Fat 11.5g, of which saturates 3.8g; Cholesterol 60mg; Calcium 134mg; Fibre 1g; Sodium 251mg

Laverbread cakes and bacon

Laverbread forms an integral part of the full Welsh breakfast – a small spoonful gives a subtle taste of the sea. Here, it is combined with oatmeal and shaped into small cakes. *Bara lawr a bacwn* taste best when cooked in bacon fat. Grilled tomatoes and flat mushrooms make ideal accompaniments, as do sausages and eggs.

Serves 4

200g/7oz laverbread

70g/2½oz/½ cup fine oatmeal

10ml/2 tsp fresh lemon juice

10ml/2 tsp oil

8 bacon rashers (strips)

salt and ground black pepper

Variation
Add about 100g/3½oz shelled cooked cockles (small clam) to the laverbread and oatmeal mixture in step 1. A little finely grated lemon rind is good, too.

1 Mix the laverbread, oatmeal and lemon juice, and season. Leave for 5 minutes.

2 Heat the oil in a pan, add the bacon and cook over medium-high heat until golden brown. Lift out and keep warm.

3 Drop spoonfuls of the laverbread mixture into the hot pan, flattening them gently with the back of the spoon. Cook over medium heat for a minute or two on each side until crisp and golden brown.

Per portion Energy 286kcal/1204kJ; Protein 14.1g; Carbohydrate 33.8g, of which sugars 1.4g; Fat 11.7g, of which saturates 3.1g; Cholesterol 23mg; Calcium 65mg; Fibre 3.7g; Sodium 923mg

Spiced roasted pumpkin

Until the early 1900s, the Gower Peninsula was the only area in Wales where pumpkins were grown. They were always favourites for making into pies and pickles. Here chunks of pumpkin are roasted with spices and herbs before being topped with cheese. Serve with a salad of watercress and baby spinach leaves. Minus the cheese, *Pwmpen sbeislyd wedi rhostio* makes a good accompaniment to roast meats, sausages or lamb chops.

Serves 3-4

5ml/1 tsp fennel seeds

30ml/2 tbsp olive oil

1 garlic clove, crushed

5ml/1 tsp ground ginger

5ml/1 tsp dried thyme

pinch of chilli powder (optional)

piece of pumpkin weighing about 1.5kg/3lb 6oz

75g/3oz/¾ cup cheese, such as Caerphilly, grated

salt and ground black pepper

1 Preheat the oven to 200°C/400°F/ Gas 6. Lightly crush or bruise the fennel seeds with a pestle and mortar, a rolling pin or the back of a large spoon – this helps to release their flavour.

2 Put the oil into a large mixing bowl and stir in the fennel, garlic, ginger, thyme and chilli. Season with salt and pepper and mix well.

3 Cut the skin off the pumpkin, scrape out and discard the seeds. Cut the flesh into rough chunks of about 3.5cm/1in. Toss the chunks in the oil mixture until evenly coated, then spread them in a single layer on a large baking tray.

4 Put into the hot oven and cook for about 40 minutes or until tender and golden brown on the edges. It helps to turn them over once during cooking.

5 Sprinkle the cheese over the top and return to the oven for 5 more minutes.

6 Serve straight from the baking tray, making sure all the golden bits of cheese are scraped up with the pumpkin.

Per portion Energy 171kcal/712kJ; Protein 7.1g; Carbohydrate 8.3g, of which sugars 6.4g; Fat 12g, of which saturates 5g; Cholesterol 17mg; Calcium 238mg; Fibre 3.8g; Sodium 127mg

Onion cake

Serve this simple but delicious dish, *Teisen winwns*, with a salad accompaniment. It's particularly good alongside sausages, lamb chops or roast chicken – in fact, any roast meat. The cooking time will depend on the potatoes and how thinly they are sliced: use a food processor or mandolin (if you have one) to make paper-thin slices. The mound of potatoes will cook down to make a thick buttery cake.

Serves 6

900g/2lb new potatoes, peeled and thinly sliced

2 medium onions, very finely chopped

salt and ground black pepper

about 115g/4oz/½ cup butter

1 Preheat the oven to 190°C/375°F/ Gas 5. Butter a 20cm/8in round cake tin (pan) and line the base with a circle of baking parchment.

2 Arrange some of the potato slices evenly in the bottom of the tin and then sprinkle some of the onions over them. Season with salt and pepper. Reserve 25g/1oz/2 tbsp of the butter and dot the mixture with tiny pieces of the remaining butter.

3 Repeat these layers, using up all the ingredients and finishing with a layer of potatoes. Melt the reserved butter and brush it over the top.

4 Cover the potatoes with foil, put in the hot oven and cook for 1–1½ hours, until tender and golden. Remove from the oven and leave to stand, still covered, for 10–15 minutes..

5 Carefully turn out the onion cake on to a warmed plate and serve.

Cook's tip
If using old potatoes, cook and serve in an earthenware or ovenproof-glass dish. Then remove the cover for the final 10–15 minutes to lightly brown the top.

Per portion Energy 272kcal/1133kJ; Protein 3.5g; Carbohydrate 29.5g, of which sugars 5.8g; Fat 16.3g, of which saturates 10.1g; Cholesterol 41mg; Calcium 29mg; Fibre 2.4g; Sodium 135mg

Fish & shellfish

Wales enjoys a wonderful variety of fish from its
extensive coastline and its lakes, reservoirs and
fast-flowing rivers. From the sea comes bass, brill,
hake, herring, mackerel, monkfish, plaice, skate, sole
and turbot, as well as cockles, crabs, lobsters,
oysters, mussels, prawns and scallops. Running the
rivers are grayling, wild brown trout, salmon and
sewin, while the lakes and reservoirs offer wild
brown trout and rainbow trout.

Trout with bacon

Wrapping trout this way helps to retain moisture and adds flavour, particularly to farmed fish. If you are lucky enough to obtain wild trout you will appreciate just how well its earthy flavour works with the bacon and leek. Make sure you use dry-cure bacon for this traditional *Brithyll a bacwn*.

Serves 4

4 trout, each weighing about 225g/8oz, cleaned

small parsley sprigs

4 lemon slices plus lemon wedges to serve

8 large leek leaves

8 streaky (fatty) bacon rashers (strips), rinds removed

salt and ground black pepper

Cook's tips
• This dish is nicer to eat if the backbone is removed from the fish first – ask your fishmonger to do this. Leave the head and tail on or cut them off, as you prefer.
• Use tender leaves (layers) of leek, rather than the tough outer ones. Alternatively, soften some leaves by pouring boiling water over them and leaving them to stand for a few minutes before draining.

1 Preheat the oven to 180°C/350°F/Gas 4. Rinse the trout, inside and out, under cold running water, then pat dry with kitchen paper. Season the cavities and put a few parsley sprigs and a slice of lemon into each.

2 Wrap two leek leaves, then two bacon rashers, spiral fashion around each fish. It may be helpful to secure the ends with wooden cocktail sticks (toothpicks).

3 Lay the fish in a shallow ovenproof dish, in a single layer and side by side, head next to tail.

4 Bake for about 20 minutes, until the bacon is brown and the leeks are tender. The trout should be cooked through; check by inserting a sharp knife into the thickest part.

5 Sprinkle the remaining parsley over the trout and serve.

Per portion Energy 324kcal/1357kJ; Protein 44.4g; Carbohydrate 0.4g, of which sugars 0.3g; Fat 16.1g, of which saturates 5.1g; Cholesterol 174mg; Calcium 60mg; Fibre 0.3g; Sodium 997mg

Baked salmon with herb-and-lemon mayonnaise

Years ago it was usual to poach a whole salmon in milk. Today few modern hobs have space for a fish kettle and the salmon is more likely to be cooked in the oven. Leave the head on or take it off, as you prefer. This dish, *Eog (neu sewin) wedi pobi gyda mayonnaise dail a lemon,* can be made with either salmon or sewin and served hot or cold.

Serves 6

1.35kg/3lb fresh whole salmon or sewin (sea trout), cleaned

1 small lemon, thinly sliced

handful of parsley sprigs

salt and ground black pepper

butter or oil for greasing

For the herb-and-lemon mayonnaise

300ml/½ pint/1¼ cups mayonnaise

30ml/2 tbsp natural (plain) yogurt or single (light) cream

finely grated rind of ½ lemon

30ml/2 tbsp finely chopped fresh chives

15ml/1 tbsp finely chopped fresh parsley

squeeze of lemon juice (optional)

1 Start by preheating the oven to 180°C/350°F/Gas 4. Rinse the cleaned salmon or sewin, both inside and out, under cold running water, and then pat it dry with kitchen paper. Season the cavity with a little salt and pepper and then spread half the lemon slices and the parsley sprigs inside the fish.

2 Grease a large sheet of thick foil and lay the fish on it. Put the remaining lemon slices and parsley on top. Fold the foil over to make a loose, but secure, parcel. Put into the hot oven for 40 minutes.

3 Stir together the mayonnaise ingredients, adding lemon juice to taste.

4 Lift the fish from the oven and tear open the foil. Peel away the skin, cutting around the head and tail with a sharp knife and discarding the parsley and lemon from the top of the fish. Carefully turn the fish over and repeat with the other side.

5 Lift on to a warmed serving plate and serve the salmon with the herb-and-lemon mayonnaise.

Cook's tip
To serve the dish cold, leave the fish to cool completely in the foil parcel before removing its skin. This will help the salmon to retain maximum moisture as it cools.

Per portion Energy 551kcal/2289kJ; Protein 35.9g; Carbohydrate 1.5g, of which sugars 1.2g; Fat 44.7g, of which saturates 7.3g; Cholesterol 182mg; Calcium 84mg; Fibre 0.4g; Sodium 362mg

Pan-cooked salmon with sorrel sauce

Sorrel leaves add their lovely lemony flavour to the sauce of this *Eog wedi coginio mewn padell gyda saws suran*. In its absence (because sorrel is at its best in spring and early summer) try using tender young spinach leaves or, better still, a tablespoon or two of laverbread with a squeeze of lemon juice added.

2 Turn the fish over and continue cooking the second side for about 3 minutes until it is almost cooked through. Lift out and keep warm (the salmon will finish cooking while you make the sauce).

3 Add the sorrel to the hot pan and cook, stirring, until wilted and soft. If the sorrel gives off lots of liquid, bubble it gently until reduced to a tablespoonful or two.

4 Stir in the double cream, bring just to the boil and bubble gently for no more than 1 minute. Add seasoning to taste and serve with the salmon.

Serves 4

15g/½oz/1 tbsp butter

10ml/2 tsp olive oil

4 pieces salmon fillet, each weighing about 175g/6oz

large handful of fresh sorrel leaves (about 100g/3½oz), chopped

150ml/¼ pint/double (heavy) cream

salt and ground black pepper

1 Heat the butter and oil in a pan, add the salmon and cook over medium heat for 3–5 minutes until golden brown.

Variation
This recipe also works well with other fish, such as sewin (sea trout), trout and sea bass.

Per portion Energy 549kcal/2274kJ; Protein 36.7g; Carbohydrate 1.1g, of which sugars 1g; Fat 44.2g, of which saturates 18.1g; Cholesterol 147mg; Calcium 98mg; Fibre 0.5g; Sodium 145mg

Scallops with bacon and sage

Scallops are fished off the west coast and, in particular, off Anglesey. Their sweetness is complemented by the addition of bacon. I like to serve this dish, *Cregyn bylchog gyda bacwn a saets*, with marsh samphire when it is in season – usually June to September – when it can be found on marshy coastlines.

Serves 4 as a starter, 2 as a main course

15ml/1 tbsp olive oil

4 streaky (fatty) bacon rashers (strips), cut into 2.5cm/1in strips

2–3 fresh sage leaves, chopped

small piece of butter

8 large or 16 small scallops

15ml/1 tbsp fresh lemon juice

100ml/3½fl oz dry cider or white wine

3 Add the lemon juice and cider to the pan and, scraping up any sediment, bring just to the boil. Continue bubbling gently until the mixture has reduced to a few tablespoons of syrupy sauce.

4 Serve the scallops and bacon with the sauce drizzled over.

Cook's tips
• Scallops that are particularly large can be sliced in half so that they form two discs before cooking (cut off the corals and cook these separately in the pan).
• To prepare samphire, wash it thoroughly and pick off the soft fleshy branches, discarding the thicker woody stalks. Drop it into boiling water for just 1 minute before draining and serving.

1 Heat a frying pan and add the oil, bacon and sage. Cook over medium heat, stirring occasionally, until the bacon is golden brown. Lift out and keep warm.

2 Add the butter to the pan and when hot add the scallops. Cook for about 1 minute on each side until browned. Lift out and keep warm with the bacon.

Per portion Energy 179kcal/745kJ; Protein 15.6g; Carbohydrate 1.9g, of which sugars 0.2g; Fat 10.4g, of which saturates 3.3g; Cholesterol 42mg; Calcium 19mg; Fibre 0g; Sodium 414mg

Cockle cakes

One of the simplest ways to serve cockles is to toss them in fine oatmeal and briefly fry them. Here, they are made into *Teisenni cocos*, nicest when cooked in bacon fat, though you could of course simply fry them in oil or butter. They are particularly good topped with scrambled, poached or fried egg, or as part of a full breakfast.

Makes 4-8

125g/4½oz/1 cup plain (all-purpose) flour

1 egg

150ml/¼ pint/⅔ cup milk

ground black pepper

100g/3½oz shelled cooked cockles (small clams)

15–30ml/1–2 tbsp chopped fresh chives (optional)

6 bacon rashers (slices)

oil for cooking

1 Sift the flour into a bowl, make a well in the centre and break the egg into it.

2 Mix the egg into the flour, gradually stirring in the milk to make a smooth batter. Season with pepper and stir in the cockles and chives (if using).

3 Heat a little oil in a pan, add the bacon and fry quickly. Lift out and keep warm.

4 Add tablespoonfuls of batter to the hot bacon fat, leaving them space to spread. Cook until crisp and golden, turning over once. Drain and serve with the bacon.

Per portion Energy 137kcal/572kJ; Protein 7g; Carbohydrate 13.1g, of which sugars 1.2g; Fat 6.6g, of which saturates 1.7g; Cholesterol 40mg; Calcium 63mg; Fibre 0.5g; Sodium 322mg

Oysters grilled with a herb and cheese crust

When buying oysters that are already shucked (opened and lifted from the shells), try and retain their juices so you can spoon some back into the shells for cooking. It is also nice to put a teaspoonful of laverbread in with each oyster before adding the breadcrumb topping to the *Wystrys griliedig gyda chrwst dail a chaws.*

Serves 2

6–8 oysters

½ lemon

sweet chilli sauce (optional)

50g/2oz/1 cup fresh breadcrumbs

50g/2oz/½ cup grated hard cheese

15ml/1 tbsp finely chopped chives

15ml/1 tbsp finely chopped parsley

50g/2oz/¼ cup butter

salt and ground black pepper

1 Scrub and open the oysters. Lay them, in the deep shells, in a grill (broiler) pan and squeeze a little lemon juice on to each one. Add a tiny drop of chilli sauce to each shell, if using.

2 Preheat the grill (broiler). Mix the breadcrumbs with the cheese, herbs, and a little seasoning. Spoon the mixture on top of the oysters and dot with tiny pieces of butter.

3 Cook under the grill (not too close) for about 5 minutes, or until the topping is crisp golden brown and bubbling around the edges.

Cook's tip
To open a live oyster, hold it in a cloth firmly with one hand and, with a special pointed knife, prize open at the hinge.

Per portion Energy 433kcal/1804kJ; Protein 18.3g; Carbohydrate 21.9g, of which sugars 1g; Fat 30.4g, of which saturates 18.6g; Cholesterol 123mg; Calcium 349mg; Fibre 1g; Sodium 933mg

Mussels in cider

Mussel harvesting is concentrated around north Wales, and Conwy in particular, where there is also a mussel museum. They are delicious when steamed and lifted out of their shells, and quickly fried with bacon. Here they are cooked with a broth of cider, garlic and cream – *Cregyn gleision mewn seidr*. Serve in large shallow bowls with a chunk of bread to mop up the juices.

2 Melt the butter in a very large pan and add the leek and garlic. Cook over medium heat for about 5 minutes, stirring frequently, until very soft but not browned. Season with pepper.

3 Add the cider and immediately tip in the mussels. Cover with a lid and cook quickly, shaking the pan occasionally, until the mussels have just opened (take care not to overcook and toughen them).

4 Remove the lid, add the cream and parsley and bubble gently for a minute or two. Serve immediately in shallow bowls.

Serves 4 as a starter, 2 as a main course

1.8kg/4lb mussels in their shells

40g/1½oz/3 tbsp butter

1 leek, washed and finely chopped

1 garlic clove, finely chopped

150ml/¼ pint/⅔ cup dry (hard) cider

30–45ml/2–3 tbsp double (heavy) cream

a handful of fresh parsley, chopped

ground black pepper

1 Scrub the mussels and scrape off any barnacles. Discard those with broken shells or that refuse to close when given a sharp tap with a knife. Pull off the hairy beards with a sharp tug.

Cook's tip
Eat mussels the fun way! Use an empty shell as pincers to pick out the mussels from the other shells. Don't try to eat any whose shells have not opened during cooking.

Per portion Energy 261kcal/1092kJ; Protein 21.1g; Carbohydrate 6.5g, of which sugars 2.1g; Fat 15.6g, of which saturates 8.2g; Cholesterol 104mg; Calcium 82mg; Fibre 1g; Sodium 498mg

Cockle pie

This Pembrokeshire dish, *Pastai gocos*, is sprinkled with grated cheese and browned under the grill, though it could equally well be topped with shortcrust or puff pastry and cooked in a hot oven. Serve the former with crusty bread and the latter with a crisp salad. Make it in one large dish or in individual ones.

Serves 4 as a starter, 2 as a main dish

425ml/¾ pint/scant 2 cups milk

25g/1oz/2 tbsp butter, cut into small pieces

25g/1oz/¼ cup plain (all-purpose) flour

150–200g/5½–7oz shelled cooked cockles (small clams)

100g/3½oz/1 cup mature cheese, such as Llanboidy or Llangloffan, grated

about 60ml/4 tbsp fresh breadcrumbs

salt and ground black pepper

3 Spoon the mixture into one large dish or four individual flameproof dishes. Then toss together the remaining cheese and the breadcrumbs.

4 Sprinkle the cheese and breadcrumb mixture over the cockle sauce. Put under a hot grill (broiler) until bubbling and golden. Serve immediately.

1 To make the sauce, put the milk, butter, flour and seasoning into a pan. Over medium heat and stirring constantly with a whisk, bring to the boil and bubble gently for 2–3 minutes until thick, smooth and glossy.

2 Stir in two-thirds of the cheese. Add the cockles and bring just to the boil.

Cook's tips
• Add some chopped fresh herbs (chives or parsley are good), laverbread, softened sliced leeks or some crisp-fried bacon pieces to the white sauce.
• This dish is equally delicious made with mixed seafood, such as mussels, clams, squid and cockles.

Per portion Energy 294kcal/1231kJ; Protein 16.8g; Carbohydrate 21.6g, of which sugars 5.6g; Fat 15.7g, of which saturates 9.9g; Cholesterol 64mg; Calcium 376mg; Fibre 0.5g; Sodium 562mg

Fish pie

Pastai bysgod is a traditional fish pie, using a combination of white fish and smoked haddock, with a distinct Welsh flavour. This version uses a puff pastry topping, although of course this can easily be replaced with mashed potato if you prefer. Though optional, the addition of a little laverbread adds an extra twist of Welsh flavour.

Serves 4

225g/8oz skinless white fish, such as hake, haddock or cod

225g/8oz skinless smoked haddock or cod

425ml/¾ pint/scant 2 cups milk

25g/1oz/2 tbsp butter

25g/1oz/¼ cup plain (all-purpose) flour

good pinch of freshly grated nutmeg

1 leek, thinly sliced

200g/7oz shelled cooked cockles (small clam)

30ml/2 tbsp laverbread (optional)

30ml/2 tbsp finely chopped fresh parsley

1 sheet ready-rolled puff pastry

salt and ground black pepper

1 Preheat the oven to 200°C/400°F/ Gas 6. Put the white and smoked fish in a pan with the milk. Heat until the milk barely comes to the boil, then cover and poach gently for about 8 minutes or until the fish is just cooked.

2 Lift the fish out, reserving the liquid. Break into flakes, discarding any bones.

3 Melt the butter, stir in the flour and cook for 1–2 minutes. Remove and stir in the reserved cooking liquid. Stir over medium heat until the sauce thickens.

4 Stir in the fish flakes and their juices. Add nutmeg and season to taste.

5 Add the leek, cockles, laverbread and parsley to the sauce and spoon into a 1.2 litre/2 pint ovenproof dish.

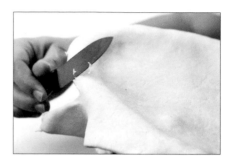

6 Brush the edges of the dish with water. Unroll the pastry and lay it over the top of the dish, trimming it to fit.

7 Use the pastry off-cuts to make decorative fish or leaves for the top, brushing each one with a little water to help them stick.

8 Put into the hot oven and cook for about 30 minutes, or until the pastry is puffed and golden brown.

Cook's tips
• If you don't have laverbread, add some shredded sorrel or some finely grated lemon rind instead.
• The puff pastry could be replaced with shortcrust pastry. Alternatively, try using several sheets of filo pastry, each lightly brushed with melted butter, either layered on top of the pie or gently scrunched up and arranged over the surface of the filling.

Per portion Energy 573kcal/2401kJ; Protein 36.8g; Carbohydrate 41g, of which sugars 7.3g; Fat 31.2g, of which saturates 4.7g; Cholesterol 92mg; Calcium 270mg; Fibre 1.2g; Sodium 1084mg

Mackerel with onions

Perhaps more than most fish, mackerel is best cooked within hours of being caught. When buying, look for really fresh fish with bright eyes and bluish-green tinges on the skin. In this recipe, *Mecryll gyda winwns*, the sweetness of the onions and the sharpness of the vinegar complement the oily flesh of the mackerel.

Serves 2

2 mackerel, cleaned

15ml/1 tbsp oil

1 large onion, very thinly sliced

1 garlic clove, finely chopped or crushed

1 bay leaf

150ml/¼ pint/⅔ cup medium apple juice or cider

30ml/2 tbsp wine vinegar

15ml/1 tbsp finely chopped fresh parsley or coriander (cilantro)

salt and ground black pepper

1 Make two or three shallow slashes down each side of each mackerel.

2 Heat the oil in a frying pan, add the mackerel and cook over medium heat for about 5–8 minutes on each side or until just cooked through. Lift out and keep warm.

3 Add the onion, garlic and bay leaf to the pan, cover and cook gently for 10–15 minutes, stirring occasionally, until soft and beginning to brown. Remove the lid, increase the heat and continue cooking until the onions are golden brown.

4 Add the apple juice and vinegar. Boil until the mixture is well reduced, thick and syrupy. Remove from the heat, stir in the parsley and seasoning to taste. Remove the bay leaf. Serve the onions with the mackerel.

Cook's tip
To serve this dish cold, flake the cooked fish, discarding skin and bones, cover with the onion mixture and leave to cool.

Per portion Energy 451kcal/1876kJ; Protein 30.5g; Carbohydrate 15.9g, of which sugars 13.5g; Fat 29.9g, of which saturates 5.6g; Cholesterol 80mg; Calcium 87mg; Fibre 2.4g; Sodium 98mg

Herrings with mustard

The west coast of Wales was famous for its herring catches, when the fish was sold door-to- door and the remainder salted and cured. Whole fish would be fried or grilled for serving with jacket potatoes, while fillets were spread with mustard, rolled and cooked with potato, onion and apple. The latter was the inspiration for this dish, *Penwaig gyda mwstard*.

Serves 2

4–6 herrings, filleted

20–30ml/4–6 tsp wholgrain mustard

4–6 small young sage leaves

1 eating apple

wholemeal (wholewheat) bread to serve

1 Preheat the oven to 190°C/350°F/ Gas 4. Rinse the herrings and dry inside and out with kitchen paper.

2 Open the fish and lay them, skin side down, on a board or the surface. Spread with 5ml/1 tsp mustard and tear 1 sage leaf over each one.

3 Quarter and core the apple and cut into thin wedges. Lay the wedges lengthways along one side of each fish, overlapping them as you go. Fold the other half of the fish over the apple.

4 Oil a baking tray (or line it with baking parchment) and carefully lift the filled herrings on to it.

5 Cook the herrings in the hot oven for about 20 minutes, until they are cooked through and just beginning to brown on the edges. Serve, freshly cooked, with wholemeal bread.

Per portion Energy 209kcal/870kJ; Protein 18.5g; Carbohydrate 3.5g, of which sugars 3.5g; Fat 13.5g, of which saturates 3.3g; Cholesterol 50mg; Calcium 102mg; Fibre 1.6g; Sodium 128mg

Meat & poultry

The Welsh diet has always relied on plentiful supplies of meat – from the days when most families fattened up a pig in the garden, cured their own bacon and kept a few hens, ducks and geese, until today, when Welsh mountain lamb and Welsh Black beef enjoy international recognition for their succulence and flavour. Wales is also proud (and justifiably so) of its saltmarsh lamb and its mountain mutton which has revived in popularity.

Lamb broth

Traditionally *Cawl Mamgu*, "granny's broth", would have been made with bony pieces of lamb and beef, usually from the neck or shin – full of flavour and cheap – and eating it would necessitate sorting through the contents and discarding bones and sinew. A large pot of cawl may well have fed a family for several days, with extra ingredients added each time it was reheated – many said that the best *cawl* was the very last bowlful.

Serves 4

30ml/2 tbsp olive oil

2 onions, roughly chopped

2 celery sticks, thickly sliced

2 carrots, thickly sliced

2 parsnips, roughly chopped

1 small swede (rutabaga), roughly chopped

800g/1¾lb lamb, such as boned shoulder, trimmed and cut into bitesize pieces

lamb or vegetable stock

30ml/2 tbsp chopped fresh thyme leaves or 10ml/2 tsp dried thyme

3 potatoes

2 leeks, trimmed

handful of chopped fresh parsley

salt and ground black pepper

1 Heat a large pan, add half the oil and stir in the onions, celery, carrots, parsnips and swede. Cook all the vegetables quickly, stirring occasionally until golden brown and then lift them out.

2 Add the remaining oil to the pan, quickly brown the lamb in batches and lift out.

3 Return the browned lamb and vegetables to the pan and pour over enough stock to cover the ingredients. Add the thyme and a little seasoning.

4 Bring to the boil and skim off any surface scum. Cover and cook gently, so that the liquid barely bubbles, for about 1½ hours, until the lamb is tender.

5 Peel and cut the potatoes into cubes and add to the pan. Cover and cook gently for 15–20 minutes until just soft.

6 Thinly slice the white part of the leeks and add to the pan, adjust the seasoning to taste and cook for 5 minutes.

7 Before serving, thinly slice the green parts of the leeks and add to the broth with the parsley. Cook for a few minutes until the leeks soften and serve.

Per portion Energy 594kcal/2488kJ; Protein 45.2g; Carbohydrate 39.4g, of which sugars 17.9g; Fat 29.6g, of which saturates 11.5g; Cholesterol 152mg; Calcium 151mg; Fibre 8.5g; Sodium 224mg

Loin of saltmarsh lamb with laverbread sauce

Laverbread goes particularly well with saltmarsh lamb. It makes a delicious sauce with milk that has been infused with vegetables and spices. The stuffing, which is made with breadcrumbs and oatmeal, is flavoured with rosemary and orange rind. *Lwyn cig oen wedi stwffio o forfa heli, gyda saws bara lawr* is good served with mixed root vegetables – such as carrots, parsnips and swede.

Serves 6

100g/3½oz dry bread

50g/2oz/½ cup fine or medium oatmeal

1 small onion, roughly chopped

5ml/1 tsp fresh rosemary leaves

grated rind of ½ orange

boned loin of saltmarsh lamb, weighing about 1kg/2¼lb

425ml/¾ pint/scant 2 cups milk

1 small onion, roughly chopped

1 small carrot, roughly chopped

1 small celery stick, roughly chopped

a few black peppercorns

a few allspice berries (optional)

1 bay leaf

30ml/2 tbsp plain (all-purpose) flour

30ml/2 tbsp laverbread

salt and ground black pepper

1 Preheat the oven to 200°C/400°F/Gas 7. Put the bread into a food processor and add the oatmeal, onion, rosemary, orange rind and seasoning. Process until finely chopped and the mixture starts to stick together. Alternatively grate the bread into fine crumbs and finely chop the onion before mixing together.

2 Open up the lamb and place on a board, skin side down. Spread the stuffing down the centre, squeezing it into a thick sausage shape. Roll the lamb back into shape to enclose the stuffing.

3 Tie securely with string in several places along the roll. Place in a medium-sized roasting tin (pan).

4 Put into the hot oven and cook for 15 minutes, then reduce the temperature to 160°C/325°F/Gas 3 and cook for a further 30–40 minutes or until the lamb is cooked to your liking.

5 Meanwhile, put the milk in a pan with the onion, carrot, celery, peppercorns, allspice (if using) and bay leaf. Heat slowly and, as soon as the milk boils, remove from the heat and leave to stand for the flavours to infuse for at least 15 minutes.

6 When the lamb is cooked, lift it out and leave in a warm place to rest for 15 minutes.

7 Pour any excess fat from the tin, leaving 15–30ml/1–2 tbsp. Strain the milk into the tin and, with a whisk, stir in the flour. Cook over medium heat, stirring with the whisk, until the sauce thickens and comes to the boil. Stir in the laverbread and bubble gently for a minute or two.

8 Adjust the seasoning, and add any juices that may have seeped from the lamb. Serve the lamb with the sauce.

Per portion Energy 406kcal/1704kJ; Protein 36.4g; Carbohydrate 21.6g, of which sugars 2.9g; Fat 20g, of which saturates 8.8g; Cholesterol 127mg; Calcium 77mg; Fibre 2.1g; Sodium 256mg

Lamb with honey, rosemary and cider

Welsh mountain lamb with honey and rosemary are traditional partners. Here, in *Cig oen gyda mêl, rhosmari a seidr*, they are teamed with cider and cooked until the lamb is meltingly soft and the sweet juices are caramelized and golden. There are several cider producers operating in Wales today, concentrated mainly in the south-east. Every year the Welsh Cider Festival is held in the City Hall, Cardiff.

Serves 4–6

1.5kg/3lb 6oz shoulder of lamb

2 garlic cloves, halved

fresh rosemary sprigs

75ml/5 tbsp clear honey

300ml/½ pint/1¼ cups dry (hard) cider, plus extra if necessary

lemon juice (optional)

salt and ground black pepper

1 Preheat the oven to 220°C/425°F/Gas 7. Rub the lamb with the cut garlic. Put the meat and the garlic in a deep roasting tin (pan). Season with salt and pepper.

2 Make small slashes in the meat with a knife and push in a few small sprigs of rosemary.

3 Stir the honey into the cider until it has fully dissolved and then pour it over the lamb.

4 Put the roasting tin into the hot oven and cook the lamb for 20–30 minutes until it has browned and the juices have reduced, begun to caramelize and turn golden brown. Keep checking to make sure the liquid does not dry up and brown too much.

5 Stir 300ml/½ pint water into the pan juices and spoon them over the lamb. Cover with a large tent of foil, scrunching the edges around the rim of the tin to seal them. Then put the pan back into the oven, reduce the temperature to 180°C/350°F/Gas 4 and cook for about another hour.

6 Remove the foil and spoon the juices over the lamb again. Turn the oven temperature back up to 220°C/425°F/Gas 7 and continue cooking, uncovered, for a further 10–15 minutes, until the lamb is crisp and brown.

7 Lift the lamb on to a serving plate and leave in a warm place to rest for 15 minutes before carving.

8 While the lamb is resting, spoon any excess fat off the top of the juices in the tin. Then taste the juices and adjust the seasoning, if necessary, adding lemon juice to taste. Put the roasting tin on the hob and bring just to the boil.

9 Serve the carved lamb with the juices spooned over.

Cook's tip
Though it looks attractive when the rosemary stands proud of the lamb, it is likely to burn. So make sure the slashes are deep and that you push the rosemary sprigs into the lamb.

Variation
Apple juice, light vegetable stock or water could be used in place of cider.

Per portion Energy 524kcal/2180kJ; Protein 35.3g; Carbohydrate 10.9g, of which sugars 10.9g; Fat 36.5g, of which saturates 17g; Cholesterol 153mg; Calcium 17mg; Fibre 0g; Sodium 130mg

Minted lamb with leeks and honey

Mint, together with thyme and savory, have always been significant culinary herbs in Wales and mint's particular affinity with lamb is indisputable. In Welsh, this dish is known as *Cig oen â mintys gyda chennin a mêl.* The lamb is marinated in a mixture of oil, lemon juice and mint before it is pan-fried.

2 Heat a frying pan and add the remaining oil and the lamb. Cook over medium heat for 6–8 minutes each side or until browned and cooked to your liking. Lift out and keep warm.

3 Drain off any excess fat from the pan, leaving about 15ml/1 tbsp. Add the leeks and garlic, and scrape up any sediment from the base of the pan. Cover and cook over medium heat for about 5 minutes, stirring occasionally, until the leeks are soft.

Serves 2

30ml/2 tbsp olive oil

15ml/1 tbsp fresh lemon juice

30ml/2 tbsp finely chopped fresh mint leaves

4 lamb chops or steaks

250g/9oz/2 cups leeks, thinly sliced

1 garlic clove, finely chopped or crushed

45ml/3 tbsp double (heavy) cream

10ml/2 tsp clear honey

salt and ground black pepper

1 In a shallow, non-metal container, mix 15ml/1 tbsp of the oil with the lemon juice, a little seasoning and 15ml/1 tbsp of the mint. Add the lamb and turn until well coated with the mint mixture. If time allows, cover and leave to stand for 30 minutes (or longer in the refrigerator), turning the lamb over occasionally.

4 Stir in the remaining mint, cream and honey and heat gently until bubbling. Adjust the seasoning if necessary. Serve the leeks in sauce with the lamb.

Variation
This recipe also works well with rosemary instead of mint. Strip the tender young leaves from a small sprig and chop them finely.

Per portion Energy 521kcal/2166kJ; Protein 31.8g; Carbohydrate 7.9g, of which sugars 7g; Fat 40.5g, of which saturates 17g; Cholesterol 145mg; Calcium 54mg; Fibre 2.8g; Sodium 137mg

Katt pie

These delicious sweet-savoury *Pastai Katt* were traditionally made for the annual fair at Templeton in Pembrokeshire. The lamb, sugar and currants would have been layered inside pies made with suet pastry. This recipe uses a crisp shortcrust pastry made with equal quantities of lard and butter. Serve with a salad of watercress, baby spinach leaves and red onion.

Serves 6

250g/9oz/2¼ cups plain (all-purpose) flour

75g/3oz/6 tbsp chilled lard, cut into small cubes

75g/3oz/6 tbsp chilled butter, cut into small cubes

300g/11oz lean minced (ground) lamb, such as shoulder

75g/3oz/⅓ cup currants

75g/3oz/6 tbsp dark muscovado (molasses) sugar

salt and ground black pepper

milk for brushing

3 Preheat the oven to 190°C/375°F/ Gas 5. Mix together the lamb, currants and sugar with a little salt and pepper.

4 On a lightly floured surface, roll out two-thirds of the dough into a circle.

5 Use the rolled-out dough to line a 20–23cm/ 8–9in tart tin (pan). Then spread the lamb mixture over the pastry. Roll out the remaining pastry to make a lid and lay this on top of the lamb filling. Then trim off the excess pastry and pinch the edges together to seal them. Make a small slit in the centre of the pastry and then brush the top with milk.

6 Put the pie into the hot oven and cook for about 40 minutes, until the pastry is crisp and golden brown and the filling is cooked through. Serve warm or at room temperature.

1 To make the pastry, sift the flour and salt into a bowl. Add the lard and butter. With the fingertips, rub the fat into the flour until the mixture resembles fine breadcrumbs. Alternatively, you can process the mixture in a food processor.

2 Stir in about 60–75ml/4–5 tbsp cold water until the mixture can be gathered together into a smooth dough. Then wrap and refrigerate the dough for about 20–30 minutes.

Per portion Energy 527kcal/2206kJ; Protein 13.9g; Carbohydrate 54g, of which sugars 22.2g; Fat 29.9g, of which saturates 14.7g; Cholesterol 77mg; Calcium 88mg; Fibre 1.5g; Sodium 114mg

Bacon with parsley sauce

The Welsh translation of this recipe title is *Bacwn gyda saws persli.* "In the old days" bacon was extremely salty and required soaking in several changes of cold water before cooking. Today the meat can be brought to the boil in cold water and then drained. The parsley sauce used to be made not with milk but with potato water, and this might be added to the *cawl.*

Serves 6–8

piece of bacon such as corner or collar, weighing about 1.35kg/3lb

1 large onion, thickly sliced

1 large carrot, thickly sliced

2 celery sticks, roughly chopped

6 black peppercorns

4 whole cloves

2 bay leaves

600ml/1 pint/2½ cups milk

25g/1oz/2 tbsp butter

25g/1oz/¼ cup plain (all-purpose) flour

handful of fresh parsley, finely chopped

1 Put the bacon in a large pan and cover it with cold water. Bring the water slowly to the boil, then drain off and discard it. If necessary rinse the pan and replace the bacon.

2 To the bacon in the pan, add the onion, carrot, celery, peppercorns, cloves and bay leaves. Pour in enough cold water to cover the bacon by about 2.5cm (1in) or slightly more.

3 Bring slowly to the boil and, if necessary, skim any scum off the surface. Cover and simmer very gently for 1 hour 20 minutes.

4 To make the parsley sauce, put the milk, butter and flour into a pan. Stirring continuously with a whisk, cook over medium heat until the sauce thickens and comes to the boil. Stir in the parsley and let the sauce bubble gently for 1–2 minutes before seasoning to taste with salt and pepper.

5 Lift the bacon on to a warmed serving plate, cover with foil and leave to rest for 15 minutes before slicing and serving with the parsley sauce.

Cook's tip
Use the stock from the bacon to make cawl with vegetables and dried lentils, peas or beans.

Per portion Energy 467kcal/1937kJ; Protein 32.7g; Carbohydrate 5.7g, of which sugars 3.7g; Fat 34.8g, of which saturates 14.4g; Cholesterol 87mg; Calcium 118mg; Fibre 0.4g; Sodium 2045mg

Roast belly of pork with root vegetables

Nothing quite compares with the rich flavour of belly of pork, particularly when it is topped with a crisp layer of crackling. The secret with this recipe, *Bol mochyn wedi rhostio ar wely gwreiddlysiau*, is to make sure the vegetables do not dry up during roasting. Let them, and the pan juices, reach a deep golden brown before topping up with additional water.

Serves 4–6

1 small swede (rutabaga), weighing about 500g/1lb 2oz

1 onion

1 parsnip

2 carrots

15ml/1 tbsp olive oil

1.5kg/3lb 6oz belly of pork, well scored

15ml/1 tbsp fresh thyme leaves or 5ml/1 tsp dried thyme

sea salt flakes and ground black pepper

1 Preheat the oven to 220°C/425°F/ Gas 7. Cut the vegetables into small cubes (about 2cm/¾ in) and stir them with the oil in a roasting tin (pan), tossing them until evenly coated. Pour in 300ml/½ pint/1¼ cups water.

2 Sprinkle the pork rind with thyme, salt and pepper, rubbing them well into the scored slashes in the pork belly. Place the pork on top of the vegetables, pressing it down so that it sits level, with the skin side uppermost.

3 Put the pork and vegetables into the hot oven and cook for 30 minutes, by which time the liquid will have almost evaporated to leave a golden crust in the bottom of the tin.

4 Add 600ml/1 pint/2½ cups cold water to the vegetables in the tin. Reduce the oven temperature to 180°C/350°F/Gas 4, and cook for 1½ hours, or until the pork is tender and the juices run clear when the centre of the meat is pierced with a sharp knife. Check the oven during the final 30 minutes to make sure the liquid does not dry up completely, adding a little extra water if necessary.

5 If the crackling is not yet crisp enough, increase the oven temperature to 220°C/425°F/Gas7 and continue cooking for another 10–20 minutes, adding extra water if necessary – just enough to prevent the vegetables from burning on the bottom of the tin.

6 With a sharp knife, slice off the crackling. Serve it with thick slices of the pork, some vegetables and the golden juices spooned over.

Cook's tip
Ask your butcher to score (slash) the pork rind really well, or use a strong sharp blade and (with care) do it yourself.

Per portion Energy 1014kcal/4194kJ; Protein 39.5g; Carbohydrate 9.4g, of which sugars 7.3g; Fat 91.2g, of which saturates 33.1g; Cholesterol 180mg; Calcium 81mg; Fibre 3.3g; Sodium 202mg

Liver, bacon and onions

Simple yet so full of flavour, this dish, *Afu, bacwn a winwnsor* or *lau bacwn a nionod*, was traditionally made with pig's liver. Here, lamb's liver is the main ingredient, although you can use pig's liver if you prefer. Serve with creamy mashed potatoes to soak up the sauce, maybe with swede, parsnip or pumpkin added. Don't overcook the liver, as it will only toughen.

2 Heat the oil in a large frying pan and add the bacon. Cook over medium heat until the fat runs out of the bacon and it is browned and crisp. Lift out and keep warm.

3 Add the onions and sage to the frying pan. Cook over medium heat for about 10–15 minutes, stirring occasionally, until the onions are soft and golden brown. Lift out with a draining spoon and keep warm.

4 Increase the heat under the pan and, adding a little extra oil if necessary, add the liver in a single layer. Cook for 3–4 minutes, turning once, until browned both sides.

5 Return the onions to the pan and pour in the stock. Bring just to the boil and bubble gently for a minute or two, seasoning to taste with salt and pepper. Serve topped with the bacon.

Serves 4

450g/1lb lamb's liver

30ml/2 tbsp plain (all-purpose) flour

15ml/1 tbsp oil, plus extra if necessary

8 rindless streaky (fatty) bacon rashers (slices)

2 onions, thinly sliced

4 fresh small sage leaves, finely chopped

150ml/¼ pint/⅔ cup chicken or vegetable stock

salt and ground black pepper

1 Pat the liver with kitchen paper, then trim it and, with a sharp knife, cut on the diagonal to make thick strips. Season the flour and toss the liver in it until it is well coated, shaking off any excess flour.

Per portion Energy 310kcal/1293kJ; Protein 28.7g; Carbohydrate 13.7g, of which sugars 5.7g; Fat 15.9g, of which saturates 4.4g; Cholesterol 500mg; Calcium 44mg; Fibre 1.6g; Sodium 400mg

Braised beef with vegetables

Stews such as *Cig eidion brwysiedig gyda llysiau* were the mainstay of the Welsh kitchen, when everything was left to cook gently all day in one large pot on the range or (in earlier times) edge of the fire. Gentle simmering in a modern oven produces an equally delicious dish. "Trollies", a form of dumpling made with oatmeal and currants, often replaced potatoes.

Serves 4–6

1kg/2¼lb lean stewing steak, cut into 5cm/2in cubes

45ml/3 tbsp plain (all-purpose) flour,

45ml/3 tbsp oil

1 large onion, thinly sliced

1 large carrot, thickly sliced

2 celery sticks, finely chopped

300ml/½ pint/¼ cup beef stock

30ml/2 tbsp tomato purée (paste)

5ml/1 tsp dried mixed herbs

15ml/1 tbsp dark muscovado (molasses) sugar

225g/8oz baby potatoes, halved

2 leeks, thinly sliced

salt and ground black pepper

1 Preheat the oven to 150°C/300°F/ Gas 2. Season the flour and use to coat the beef cubes.

2 Heat the oil in a large, flameproof casserole. Add a small batch of meat, cook quickly until browned on all sides and, with a slotted spoon, lift out. Repeat with the remaining beef.

Variation
Replace the potatoes with dumplings. Sift 175g/6oz/1½ cups self-raising (self-rising) flour and stir in 75g/3oz/½ cup shredded suet, 30ml/2 tbsp chopped parsley and season. Stir in water to make a soft dough and divide the mixture into 12 balls. In step 6, stir in the leeks and put the dumplings on top. Cover and cook for 15–20 minutes more.

3 Add the onion, carrot and celery to the casserole. Cook over medium heat for about 10 minutes, stirring frequently, until they begin to soften and brown slightly on the edges.

4 Return the meat to the casserole and add the stock, tomato purée, herbs and sugar, at the same time scraping up any sediment that has stuck to the casserole. Heat until the liquid nearly comes to the boil.

5 Cover with a tight fitting lid and put into the hot oven. Cook for 2–2½ hours, or until the beef is tender.

6 Gently stir in the potatoes and leeks, cover and continue cooking for a further 30 minutes or until the potatoes are soft.

Per portion Energy 450kcal/1880kJ; Protein 41.3g; Carbohydrate 23.6g, of which sugars 10.3g; Fat 21.7g, of which saturates 7.3g; Cholesterol 97mg; Calcium 63mg; Fibre 3.5g; Sodium 137mg

Bacon, chicken and leek pudding

Old-fashioned suet puddings are still a favourite, and this one, *Pwdin bacwn, cyw a chennin,* is bursting with flavour. The pastry is quite thin, but to make it thicker, simply increase the flour to 225g/8oz/2 cups and the suet to 100g/3½oz/⅔ cup. Serve it with seasonal vegetables or a green salad tossed lightly in an oil and vinegar dressing.

Serves 4

200g/7oz unsmoked lean, rindless bacon, preferably in one piece

400g/14oz skinless boneless chicken, preferably thigh meat

2 small or medium leeks, finely chopped

30ml/2 tbsp finely chopped fresh parsley

175g/6oz/1¼ cups self-raising (self-rising) flour

75g/3oz/½ cup shredded suet

120ml/4fl oz chicken or vegetable stock, or water

ground black pepper

butter for greasing

1 Cut the bacon and chicken into bitesize pieces into a large bowl. Mix them with the leeks and half the parsley. Season with black pepper.

2 Sift the flour into another large bowl and stir in the suet and the remaining parsley. With a round-bladed knife, stir in sufficient cold water to make a soft dough. On a lightly floured surface, roll out the dough to a circle measuring about 33cm/13in across. Cut out one quarter of the circle (starting from the centre, like a wedge), roll up and reserve.

3 Lightly butter a 1.2 litre/2 pint pudding bowl. Use the rolled out dough to line the buttered bowl, pressing the cut edges together to seal them and allowing the pastry to overlap the top of the bowl slightly.

4 Spoon the bacon and chicken mixture into the lined bowl, packing it neatly and taking care not to split the pastry. Pour the chicken or vegetable stock over the bacon mixture making sure it does not overfill the bowl.

5 Roll out the reserved pastry into a circle to form a lid and lay it over the filling, pinching the edges together to seal them well. Cover with baking parchment (pleated in the centre to allow the pudding to rise) and then a large sheet of foil (again pleated at the centre). Tuck the edges under and press them tightly to the sides of the bowl until well sealed.

6 Steam the pudding over boiling water for about 3½ hours. Check the water level occasionally. Uncover the pudding, slide a knife around the sides and turn out on to a warmed serving plate.

Per portion Energy 535kcal/2236kJ; Protein 28.2g; Carbohydrate 39.4g, of which sugars 2.9g; Fat 31.3g, of which saturates 14.8g; Cholesterol 86mg; Calcium 111mg; Fibre 4g; Sodium 999mg

Oven-cooked potatoes with bacon

This Carmarthenshire dish, *Tatw rhost a bacwn*, is often called Miser's Feast. Originally, the potatoes, onions and slices of bacon would have been layered in the cooking pot with water and then cooked over an open fire. Here, a flameproof casserole is put on the hob to brown chopped bacon and soften the vegetables before adding stock and putting it in the oven. You could also use a large frying pan and then transfer everything to an ovenproof casserole. Serve with a crisp salad or stir-fried vegetables, or as an accompaniment to grilled sausages.

Serves 4

15ml/1 tbsp oil

25g/1oz/2 tbsp butter

8 thick rindless bacon rashers (strips), chopped

2 onions, thinly sliced

1kg/2¼lb potatoes (about 3 large), thinly sliced

600ml/1 pint/2½ cups stock – chicken or vegetable stock (or a mixture)

ground black pepper

chopped fresh parsley, to garnish

1 Preheat the oven to 190°C/ 375°F/Gas 5. Heat the oil and butter in a wide flameproof casserole, add the bacon and cook over medium heat, stirring occasionally, until the bacon is just beginning to brown at its edges.

2 The next stage is to add the thinly sliced onions to the bacon in the casserole. Cook for 5–10 minutes, stirring occasionally, until the onions have slightly softened and turned a rich golden brown.

3 Add the potatoes and stir well. Pour in the stock and level the surface, pushing the potatoes and onions into the liquid. Season with black pepper.

4 Bring to the boil, cover and put into the hot oven. Cook for 30–40 minutes or until the vegetables are soft.

5 Remove the cover. Raise the oven temperature to 220°C/425°F/Gas 7 and cook for a further 15–20 minutes, until the top is crisp and golden brown. Garnish with some chopped parsley.

Variation
Try adding a little chopped fresh sage, shredded wild garlic or leeks, or some grated mature cheese in step 4.

Per portion Energy 385kcal/1615kJ; Protein 14.8g; Carbohydrate 48.2g, of which sugars 8.9g; Fat 16.1g, of which saturates 7.1g; Cholesterol 43mg; Calcium 44mg; Fibre 3.9g; Sodium 935mg

Roast chicken with leek, laver and lemon stuffing

The three "Ls" – leek, laver and lemon – complement each other beautifully to make a light stuffing that goes perfectly with chicken. You can also add finely grated cheese. In Welsh, this dish is known as *Ffowlyn rhost gyda stwffin cennin, lafwr a lemon.*

Serves 4–6

1.4–1.8kg/3–4lb oven-ready chicken

1 small onion, quartered

½ lemon, roughly chopped

2 garlic cloves, halved

olive oil or melted butter

For the stuffing

30ml/2 tbsp olive oil

2 rindless bacon rashers (slices), finely chopped

1 small leek, thinly sliced

1 garlic clove, crushed or finely chopped

30ml/2 tbsp laverbread

150g/5½oz/1¼ cups fresh breadcrumbs

finely grated rind and juice of ½ lemon

salt and ground black pepper

1 To make the stuffing, put the oil and bacon into a pan and cook over medium heat, stirring occasionally, for about 3 minutes without browning. Add the leek and garlic and cook for 3–5 minutes, stirring occasionally, until soft and just beginning to brown. Remove from the heat and stir in the laverbread, breadcrumbs, lemon rind and juice, and seasoning. Leave to cool.

Cook's tip
The stuffing is also excellent for spooning under the skin of chicken breasts, or piling on to fillets of fish before oven cooking.

2 Preheat the oven to 200°C/400°F/Gas 6. Rinse the chicken inside and out, and then pat dry with kitchen paper. Spoon the cooled stuffing into the neck cavity of the chicken and fold the skin over and under. Any excess stuffing can be put under the breast skin – loosen it carefully by sliding your fingers underneath and then fill the resulting pocket evenly.

3 Put the onion, lemon and garlic into the main cavity of the chicken. Sit the bird in a roasting tin (pan) and brush it all over with olive oil or melted butter. Cover the breast area with a small piece of foil.

4 Put into the hot oven and cook for about 1½ hours, or until the chicken is cooked through (when a sharp knife is inserted in the thick part of the thigh next to the breast, the juices should run clear, not pink). Remove the foil for the final 30 minutes of cooking to allow the skin to brown and crisp.

5 Remove from the oven and leave to rest in a warm place for 15–20 minutes before carving. Reheat the pan juices and serve them spooned over the chicken.

Per portion Energy 486kcal/2027kJ; Protein 33.4g; Carbohydrate 22.3g, of which sugars 1.2g; Fat 29.7g, of which saturates 8.1g; Cholesterol 154mg; Calcium 54mg; Fibre 1g; Sodium 461mg

Chicken and leek pies

Make these individual pies, or *Pasteiod ffowlyn a chennin*, in small tart tins or in a four-hole Yorkshire pudding tin. Alternatively, as in the main picture, make one large pie using a 20cm/8in tart tin or pie plate. These are good served hot, warm or cold and are ideal for picnics.

Serves 4

400g/14oz shortcrust pastry, thawed if frozen

15g/½oz/1 tbsp butter

1 leek, thinly sliced

2 eggs

225g/8oz skinless chicken breast fillets, finely chopped

small handful of fresh parsley or mint, finely chopped

salt and ground black pepper

beaten egg, to glaze

1 Preheat the oven to 200°C/400°F/ Gas 6.Roll out the pastry on a lightly floured surface to a thickness of about 3mm/⅛in. Cut out four circles, each large enough to line an individual tart tin (pan) and line the four pans. Cut the remaining pastry into four slightly smaller circles ready to make lids for the pies.

2 Melt the butter in a small pan, add the leek and cook gently for about 5 minutes, stirring occasionally, until soft but not brown.

3 Beat the eggs in a bowl and stir in the chicken, herbs and seasoning. Add the leek and its buttery juices from the pan, stirring until well mixed.

4 Spoon the mixture into the pastry cases, filling them generously. Brush the edges of the pastry with beaten egg and place the lids on top, pressing the edges together to seal them. Brush the tops of the pies with beaten egg and make a small slit in the centre of each to allow steam to escape.

5 Put into the hot oven and cook for about 30 minutes, until golden brown and cooked through.

Variation
The pies are just as nice made with puff pastry instead of shortcrust.

Per portion Energy 588kcal/2459kJ; Protein 23.4g; Carbohydrate 48.4g, of which sugars 2.1g; Fat 34.9g, of which saturates 11.7g; Cholesterol 157mg; Calcium 133mg; Fibre 3.4g; Sodium 496mg

Faggots with onion gravy

In the days when most households reared a pig at the bottom of the garden, these *Ffagod* were made with the fresh liver on slaughter day. The paté-like mixture was wrapped in the lacy netting of the pig's caul, which held the contents together during the cooking process. In this recipe, *Ffagots a grefi nionod/winwns*, beaten egg binds the mixture. Serve the faggots with peas.

Serves 4

450g/1lb pig's liver, trimmed and roughly chopped

300g/11oz belly pork, roughly chopped

2 onions, roughly chopped

100g/3½oz/1 cup fresh breadcrumbs

1 egg, beaten

2 sage leaves, chopped

5ml/1 tsp salt

2.5ml/½ tsp ground mace

1.5ml/¼ tsp ground black pepper

150ml/¼ pint/⅔ cup beef or vegetable stock

butter for greasing

For the onion gravy:

50g/2oz/¼ cup butter

4 onions (white, red or a mixture), thinly sliced

generous 10ml/2 tsp sugar

15ml/1 tbsp plain (all-purpose) flour

300ml/½ pint/1¼ cups good beef stock

300ml/½ pint/1¼ cups good vegetable stock

salt and black pepper

1 Preheat the oven to 180°C/350°F/Gas 4. Put the liver, pork and onions in a food processor and process until finely chopped. Then turn the mixture out into a large mixing bowl and stir in the breadcrumbs, egg, sage, salt, mace and pepper until thoroughly combined.

2 With wet hands, shape the mixture into 10–12 round faggots and lay them in a shallow ovenproof dish. Pour in the stock.

3 Use a buttered sheet of foil to cover the dish, butter side down. Crimp the edges around the dish to seal them.

4 Cook in the oven for 45–50 minutes (the juices should run clear when the faggots are pierced with a sharp knife).

5 For the onion gravy, melt the butter in a large pan and add the onions and sugar. Cover and cook gently for at least 30 minutes, until the onions are soft and evenly caramelized to a rich golden brown.

6 Stir in the flour, remove from the heat and stir in both types of stock. Return the pan to the heat and, stirring continuously, bring just to the boil. Simmer gently for 20-30 minutes, stirring occasionally (if the liquid looks like reducing too much, add a splash of water). Season to taste with salt and pepper.

7 Once cooked, remove the foil covering the faggots and increase the oven temperature to 200°C/400°F/Gas 6. Cook for a further 10 minutes until lightly browned. Serve with the onion gravy.

Per portion Energy 664kcal/2768kJ; Protein 41.4g; Carbohydrate 31.2g, of which sugars 9.8g; Fat 42.5g, of which saturates 17.9g; Cholesterol 421mg; Calcium 84mg; Fibre 2.2g; Sodium 434mg

Duck with damson and ginger sauce

Probably the most celebrated duck dish in Wales must be Lady Llanover's 19th-century recipe, which involved salting a whole bird for three days before cooking. Slices of the cold salt duck were often served with a sharp-tasting fruit sauce of damsons, plums or whinberries. Simple pan-fried duck breasts go well with a fruit sauce too, as in this recipe, *Brestiau hwyaid gyda saws eirin duon mawr a sinsir*.

Serves 4

250g/9oz fresh damsons

5ml/1 tsp ground ginger

45ml/3 tbsp sugar

10ml/2 tsp wine vinegar or sherry vinegar

4 duck breast portions

15ml/1 tbsp oil

salt and ground black pepper

1 Put the damsons in a pan with the ginger and 45ml/3 tbsp water. Bring to the boil, cover and simmer gently for about 5 minutes, or until the fruit is soft. Stir frequently and add a little extra water if the fruit looks as if it is drying out or sticking to the bottom of the pan

2 Stir in the sugar and vinegar. Press the mixture through a sieve to remove stones (pits) and skin. Taste the sauce and add more sugar (if necessary) and seasoning to taste.

3 Meanwhile, with a sharp knife, score the fat on the duck breast portions in several places without cutting into the meat. Brush the oil over both sides of the duck. Sprinkle a little salt and pepper on the fat side only.

3 Preheat a griddle pan or heavy frying pan. When hot, add the duck breast portions, skin side down, and cook over medium heat for about 5 minutes or until the fat is evenly browned and crisp. Turn over and cook the meat side for 4–5 minutes. Lift out and leave to rest for 5–10 minutes.

4 Slice the duck on the diagonal and serve with the sauce.

Cook's tip
Both the duck and the sauce are good served cold too. Serve with simple steamed vegetables or crisp salads.

Per portion Energy 275kcal/1157kJ; Protein 29.9g; Carbohydrate 17.5g, of which sugars 17.5g; Fat 12.5g, of which saturates 2.4g; Cholesterol 165mg; Calcium 39mg; Fibre 1.1g; Sodium 167mg

Roast duck with apples

Apple makes a delicious accompaniment to both duck and goose, helping to offset their rich flavour. *Hwyaden wedi rhostio gydag afalau* is a dish for any time of year while goose (in season September to December) has always been a meal for special occasions – New Year's Day, Michaelmas Day and more recently Christmas. The goose goes far back into the history of Wales, even having a mention in the 10th-century *Laws of Hywel Dda*. The duck is particularly famous in the mid-Wales town of Presteigne, where a trial for duck-stealing in 1857 is recreated in The Judge's Lodging Victorian Museum.

Serves 6

20g/¾oz/1½ tbsp butter

1 onion, finely chopped

5ml/1 tsp finely chopped fresh sage or 2.5ml/½ tsp dried

75g/3oz/1½ cups fresh breadcrumbs

1 oven-ready duck, weighing about 1.8–2.25kg/4–5lb

3 crisp eating apples

salt and ground black pepper

1 To make the stuffing melt the butter in a pan, add the onion and cook gently for about 5 minutes, stirring occasionally, until soft but not browned. Then remove from the heat and stir in the sage, breadcrumbs, salt and pepper.

2 Preheat the oven to 200C/400F/ Gas 6. Remove any lumps of fat from inside the duck. With a fork, prick the skin all over then rub it all over with salt.

3 Spoon the stuffing into the neck end of the bird and, with a small skewer, secure the skin over the opening.

4 Sit the duck on a rack in a roasting tin (pan) and pour in 150ml/¼ pint/⅔ cup cold water. Cover the breast area of the duck with foil. Roast in the hot oven for 30 minutes.

5 Lift the duck and the rack out of the tin and drain off excess fat, leaving a little fat, all the sediment and juices.

6 Quarter and core the apples and cut them into thick wedges.

7 Add the wedges to the roasting tin, stirring until they are all evenly coated with fat and juices.

8 Replace the duck on the rack over the apples. Continue cooking for 30 minutes, turning the apples over once, until the duck is crisp, golden brown and cooked through. Check by inserting a skewer into the thickest part of the leg next to the breast – the juices should run clear.

9 Before carving, leave the duck in warm place to rest for 10–15 minutes.

Variation for cooking goose:
The goose goes far back into the history of Wales, with even a mention in the *Laws of Hywel Dda*. This variation adapts the quantities and method to suit goose.
• When buying a goose, allow about 675g/1½lb per person – a bird weighing about 5.5kg/12lb will feed eight.
• For eight servings, make twice as much stuffing and use about 6 apples.
• Prick the skin of the goose all over with a fork or skewer – try not to pierce the meat beneath.
• Any fat removed from the cavity can be placed on the breast of the goose before covering with foil and cooking.
• Cook at 190°C/375°F/Gas 5.
• A 5.5kg/12lb goose will take about 2½–3 hours to cook. Check it is cooked through by inserting a skewer into the thickest part of the leg next to the breast – the juices should run clear.
• Before carving, leave the goose in a warm place to rest for 20 minutes.
• Lots of fat will drain off the goose during cooking. Save it for roasting potatoes. It freezes well packed in small polythene boxes or freezer bags.

Per portion Energy 270kcal/1138kJ; Protein 23.7g; Carbohydrate 23.3g, of which sugars 6g; Fat 9.9g, of which saturates 3.9g; Cholesterol 119mg; Calcium 51mg; Fibre 1.6g; Sodium 303mg

Puddings

The Welsh will readily extol the virtues of simple, traditional puddings made with milk or fruit. Rice pudding is a classic example, which once held pride of place at the end of every Sunday dinner. Another much-loved Welsh pudding is fruit pie, made with apples, plums, damsons, gooseberries, rhubarb, or the constant favourite of the region, whinberries. Before ovens were invented, puddings were cooked on a flat bakestone over the fire.

Whinberry and apple tart

The traditional wild harvest of whinberries or, as many Welsh people insist, "whimberries", has always been gathered with great excitement from the hillsides in summer. The berries (elsewhere called bilberries, blueberries or whortleberries) were most often made into tarts, such as this *Tarten lus ac afalau*. It was customary to first bake the tart before carefully lifting the lid, adding the sugar and putting it all back together again. Incidentally, in Wales a tart is a tart (never a pie) even when it has pastry top and bottom.

Serves 6

2 cooking apples, total weight about 400g/14oz

10ml/2 tsp cornflour (cornstarch)

350g/12oz/3 cups whinberries

40–50g/3–4 tbsp caster (superfine) sugar, plus extra for sprinkling

milk for brushing

For the pastry

250g/9oz/2¼ cups plain (all-purpose) flour

25g/1oz/2 tbsp caster (superfine) sugar

150g/5oz/10 tbsp butter, chilled and cut into small cubes

1 egg

1 Sift the flour into a bowl and stir in the sugar. Add the butter and rub into the flour until the mixture resembles fine crumbs. Stir in the egg and enough cold water until the mixture forms clumps, then gather it together to make a smooth dough. Wrap the pastry and refrigerate for 20–30 minutes.

2 Preheat the oven to 190°C/375°F/ Gas 5. On a lightly floured surface, roll out half the dough to make a circle and use it to line a deep 23cm/9in tart tin (pan) or ovenproof dish, gently pressing it into the corners and allowing the pastry to hang over the sides slightly. Roll out the remaining pastry to a circle large enough to make a lid and check it for size.

3 Peel the apples, remove their cores and chop them into small pieces. Toss the apple pieces with the cornflour until evenly coated and arrange them in the bottom of the pastry case. Scatter the whinberries (or blueberries) on top and sprinkle the sugar over. Lightly brush the edges of the pastry with water.

4 Lay the pastry lid over the fruit filling. Trim off the excess pastry and pinch the edges together to seal them well. Make a small slit in the centre, then brush the top with milk and sprinkle with a little sugar.

5 Put into the hot oven and cook for 30–40 minutes until the pastry is crisp and golden brown and the filling is cooked through. While the pastry is still hot, sprinkle with more caster sugar.

Cook's tip
Whinberries give out a lot of juice, so don't be tempted to use a loose-bottomed tin (pan) in case it leaks out and over the floor of the oven.

Per portion Energy 403kcal/1688kJ; Protein 5.76g; Carbohydrate 51.4g, of which sugars 18.15g; Fat 20.8g, of which saturates 12.5g; Cholesterol 81.5mg; Calcium 98.6mg; Fibre 3,5g; Sodium 157.5mg

Snowdon pudding

Reminiscent of a snow-capped mountain, this light pudding was allegedly created for a hotel situated at the base of Wales' highest peak. Use the softest, juiciest raisins you can find – they are more likely to stick to the basin than small dry ones. *Pwdin Eryri* is often served with a wine sauce – to make it, simply replace the milk with white wine.

Serves 6

15–25g/½–1oz/1–2 tbsp butter, softened

100g/3½oz/⅔ cup raisins

175g/6oz/3 cups fresh white breadcrumbs

75g/3oz/½ cup shredded suet (US chilled, grated shortening)

75g/3oz/6 tbsp soft brown sugar

25g/1oz/¼ cup cornflour (cornstarch)

finely grated rind of 1 lemon

2 eggs

60ml/4 tbsp orange marmalade

30ml/2 tbsp fresh lemon juice

For the sauce:

1 lemon

25g/1oz/¼ cup cornflour (cornstarch)

300ml/½ pint/1¼ cups milk

50g/2oz/¼ cup caster (superfine) sugar

25g/1oz/2 tbsp butter

2 Mix together the breadcrumbs, suet, brown sugar, cornflour, lemon rind and the remaining raisins. Beat the eggs with the marmalade and lemon and stir into the dry ingredients.

3 Spoon the mixture into the bowl, without disturbing the raisins.

4 Cover with baking parchment (pleated) and then a large sheet of foil (also pleated). Tuck the edges under and press tightly to the sides. Steam over a pan of boiling water for 1¾ hours.

5 Pare two or three large strips of lemon rind and put into a pan with 150ml/¼ pint/⅔ cup water. Bring to the boil and simmer for 10 minutes. Discard the rind. Blend the cornflour with the milk and stir into the pan. Squeeze the juice from half the lemon and add to the pan with the sugar and butter. Heat until the sauce thickens and comes to the boil.

6 Turn the pudding out on to a warmed plate, spooning a little sauce over the top.

1 Smear the butter on the inside of a 1.2-litre/2-pint pudding bowl and press half the raisins on the buttered surface.

Per portion Energy 456kcal/1922kJ; Protein 7.7g; Carbohydrate 74.4g, of which sugars 43.4g; Fat 16.8g, of which saturates 8.6g; Cholesterol 82mg; Calcium 131mg; Fibre 1.1g; Sodium 304mg

Monmouth pudding

Another dessert with bread as a main ingredient, *Pwdin Mynwy* or Monmouth Pudding is very similar to the English Queen of Puddings. Here, red jam is layered with milk-drenched breadcrumbs, set with eggs; in the English version, the egg whites are whisked into meringue and cooked on top of the breadcrumb and jam layers.

Serves 4

425ml/¾ pint/scant 2 cups milk

25g/1oz/2 tbsp caster (superfine) sugar

finely grated rind of 1 lemon

175g/6oz/3 cups fresh white breadcrumbs

2 eggs, separated

60ml/4 tbsp strawberry, raspberry or other red jam

1 Pour the milk into a pan, add the sugar and lemon rind and bring to the boil. Pour the hot milk mixture over the breadcrumbs and leave for 15 minutes.

2 Preheat the oven to 150°C/300°F/ Gas 2. Butter a 23cm/9in ovenproof dish.

3 Stir the egg yolks into the breadcrumb mixture. Whisk the egg whites until stiff peaks form and, with a large metal spoon, fold them into the breadcrumb mixture.

4 Melt the jam (on the hob or in the microwave) and drizzle half of it into the bottom of the prepared dish.

5 Spoon half the breadcrumb mixture on top, gently levelling the surface and drizzle the jam over it.

6 Spread the remaining breadcrumb mixture over the top of the pudding to make an even layer. Put into the hot oven and cook for about 30–40 minutes or until light golden brown on top and set throughout. Serve warm.

Cook's tips
• Cooking the pudding in an ovenproof glass dish shows off the pudding's layers.
• The jam layers could be replaced with lightly cooked summer berries or plums.

Per portion Energy 309kcal/1313kJ; Protein 12g; Carbohydrate 57.1g, of which sugars 24.3g; Fat 5.4g, of which saturates 1.9g; Cholesterol 101mg; Calcium 205mg; Fibre 1g; Sodium 418mg

Apple pudding

In rural areas of southeast Wales, most homes would have had an apple tree in the back garden, often alongside damsons, plums or medlars. The fruits would be made into puddings such as *Pwdin afalau*, cakes and preserves. Today old-fashioned, single-variety apple crops are being made into preserves and the fruit is being made into award-winning apple juices.

2 Put the milk, butter and flour in a pan. Stirring continuously with a whisk, cook over medium heat until the sauce thickens and comes to the boil. Let it bubble gently for 1–2 minutes, stirring well to make sure it does not stick and burn on the bottom of the pan. Pour into a bowl, add the sugar and vanilla extract, and then stir in the egg yolks.

3 In a separate bowl, whisk the egg whites until stiff peaks form. With a large metal spoon fold the egg whites into the custard. Pour the custard mixture over the apples in the dish.

4 Put into the hot oven and cook for about 40 minutes until puffed up, deep golden brown and firm to the touch.

5 Serve straight out of the oven, before the soufflé-like topping begins to fall.

Serves 4

4 crisp eating apples

a little lemon juice

300ml/½ pint/1¼ cups milk

40g/1½oz/3 tbsp butter

40g/1½oz/⅓ cup plain (all-purpose) flour

25g/1oz/2 tbsp caster (superfine) sugar

2.5ml/½ tsp vanilla extract

2 eggs, separated

1 Preheat the oven to 200°C/400°F/ Gas 6. Butter a dish measuring 20–23cm/8–9in diameter and 5cm/2in deep. Peel, core and slice the apples and put in the dish.

Variation
Stewed fruit, such as cooking apples, plums, rhubarb or gooseberries sweetened with honey or sugar, would also make a good base for this pudding, as would fresh summer berries (blackberries, raspberries, redcurrants and blackcurrants).

Per portion Energy 240kcal/1006kJ; Protein 7g; Carbohydrate 26.8g, of which sugars 19.2g; Fat 12.5g, of which saturates 6.8g; Cholesterol 121mg; Calcium 127mg; Fibre 1.9g; Sodium 131mg

Gooseberry fool

This quickly made dessert, *Ffwl eirin Mair*, never fails to impress. Blackberries, raspberries, blackcurrants or rhubarb work well in place of gooseberries. When using young pink rhubarb there is no need to sieve the cooked fruit, so give step 2 a miss. Serve in pretty glasses with small crisp biscuits to provide a contrast in texture.

Serves 4

450g/1lb gooseberries, cut into short lengths

125g/4½oz/¼ cup caster (superfine) sugar, or to taste

300ml/½ pint/1¼ cups double (heavy) cream

1 Put the gooseberries into a pan with 30ml/2 tbsp water. Cover and cook gently for about 10 minutes until the fruit is soft. Stir in the sugar to taste.

2 Tip the fruit into a nylon sieve and press through. Leave the purée to cool.

3 Whip the cream until stiff enough to hold soft peaks. Stir in the gooseberry purée without over-mixing (it looks pretty with some streaks).

4 Spoon the mixture into serving glasses and refrigerate until required.

Per portion Energy 517kcal/2147kJ; Protein 2.6g; Carbohydrate 37.3g, of which sugars 37.3g; Fat 40.7g, of which saturates 25.1g; Cholesterol 103mg; Calcium 85mg; Fibre 2.7g; Sodium 21mg

Bread pudding

Welsh cooks, just like those in other parts of Britain, were extremely inventive with the stale ends of loaves and bread pudding, or *Pwdin bara,* is one example. This dish is spicy, rich and filling – and is therefore an ideal winter food. Serve the pudding warm with custard or cream, or if you prefer it's just as nice left until cold.

Makes 9 squares

225g/8oz/4 cups stale bread, weighed after removing crusts

300ml/½ pint/1¼ cups milk

butter, for greasing

50g/1¾oz/4 tbsp dark muscovado (molasses) sugar

85g/3oz/½ cup shredded suet (US chilled, grated shortening) or grated chilled butter

225g/8oz/1⅓ cups mixed dried fruit, including currants, sultanas (golden raisins), finely chopped citrus peel

15ml/1 tbsp mixed (apple pie) spice

2.5ml/½ tsp freshly grated nutmeg

finely grated rind of 1 small orange and 1 small lemon, plus a little orange or lemon juice

1 egg, lightly beaten

caster (superfine) sugar for sprinkling

3 Using a fork, break up the bread before stirring in the sugar, suet, dried fruit, spices and citrus rinds. Beat in the egg, adding some orange or lemon juice to make a soft mixture.

Cook's tip
Although suet is traditional, you may prefer to use grated chilled butter.

4 Spread the mixture into the prepared dish and level the surface.

5 Put into the hot oven and cook for about 1¼ hours or until the top is brown and firm to the touch.

6 Sprinkle caster sugar over the surface and cool before cutting into squares.

1 Break the bread into small pieces. Place in a large mixing bowl, pour the milk over and leave for about 30 minutes.

2 Preheat the oven to 180°C/350°F/Gas 4. Butter an 18cm/7in square and 5cm/2in deep ovenproof dish.

Per portion Energy 254kcal/1072kJ; Protein 4.3g; Carbohydrate 39.7g, of which sugars 27g; Fat 10.2g, of which saturates 5.3g; Cholesterol 31mg; Calcium 103mg; Fibre 1.4g; Sodium 147mg

Chilled fruit pudding

This trifle-like dish, *Pwdin frwythau oeredig*, has overtones of Summer Pudding. A little thick natural yogurt gives a lighter touch than an all-cream topping. The Welsh have always used flowers in their cooking and the elderflower cordial adds its fragrance to the topping. Don't use processed sliced bread; a good traditional loaf will give a superior result.

Serves 4–6

550g/1lb 4oz mixed soft fruit, such as raspberries, blackberries, blackcurrants, redcurrants

50g/2oz/4 tbsp sugar

large thick slice of bread with crusts removed, about 125g/4½oz/2 cups without crusts

300ml/½ pint/1¼ cups double (heavy) cream

45ml/3 tbsp elderflower cordial

150ml/¼ pint/⅔ cup thick natural (plain) yogurt

1 Reserve a few raspberries, blackberries, blackcurrants or redcurrants for decoration, then put the remainder into a pan with the sugar and 30ml/2 tbsp water. Bring just to the boil, cover and simmer gently for 4–5 minutes until the fruit is soft and plenty of juice has formed.

2 Cut the bread into cubes, measuring about 2.5cm/1in, and put them into one large dish or individual serving bowls or glasses.

Cook's tip
A bag of mixed frozen fruit is ideal for this dessert.

3 Spoon the fruit mixture over the bread and leave to cool.

Variation
Instead of mixing yogurt into the topping, try using the same quantity of ready-made custard – it gives a richer, sweeter result.

4 Whip the cream with the cordial until stiff peaks begin to form. Gently stir in the yogurt and spoon the mixture over the top of the fruit.

5 Chill until required. Just before serving, decorate the top with the reserved fruit.

Per portion Energy 382kcal/1592kJ; Protein 5.2g; Carbohydrate 29.9g, of which sugars 20.2g; Fat 27.8g, of which saturates 16.9g; Cholesterol 69mg; Calcium 124mg; Fibre 2.6g; Sodium 144mg

Bara brith ice cream

Bara brith means "speckled bread" (see bara brith recipes on pages 80–81). This delicious ice-cream *Hufen iâ bara brith* recipe combines a teabread version of bara brith with cream, custard and brandy. It is simple to make and thoroughly decadent. Make it by hand, as in the recipe, or if you have an ice-cream machine, it's ideal for that too.

About 6–8 servings

300ml/½ pint/1¼ cups double (heavy) cream, chilled

500g/1lb 2oz carton ready-made custard, chilled

30ml/2 tbsp brandy or whisky

225g/8oz/2 cups bara brith (use the tea-bread version, see page 81)

1 Switch your freezer to its very coldest setting.

2 Tip the cream, custard and whisky into a large plastic bowl or freezer box and, with a whisk, stir well.

3 Cover and freeze for 1½–2 hours. Every 30 minutes or so take the box out of the freezer and stir well to move the ice crystals from around the edges to the centre of the bowl (you can set a timer to remind you to stir).

4 Meanwhile, crumble or chop the *bara brith* into very small pieces.

5 When the mixture is slushy, break up the ice crystals with a fork, electric hand-mixer or food processor, and quickly return it to the freezer for about 1 hour.

6 Each time the mixture thickens and becomes slushy, repeat the mashing procedure once or twice more until the ice cream is thick and creamy.

Cook's tip

For easy freezing, the individual ingredients should be well chilled before they are mixed together at step 2. So if time allows it's always a good idea to set the freezer to its coldest setting several hours earlier (or overnight) and then leave the mixed ingredients in the refrigerator to chill.

7 Stir in the crumbled or chopped bara brith, cover and freeze the ice cream until required.

Cook's tip

For vanilla custard, pour 300ml/½ pint/ 1¼ cups full cream milk into a heavy pan and add a vanilla pod (first split with the point of a sharp knife along its length and the seeds scraped straight into the milk). Bring the milk almost to the boil, remove from the heat and leave to stand for 10-20 minutes.

In a bowl, beat three large eggs with 85g/3oz/½ cup caster sugar, stir in the milk and remove the vanilla pod. Clean the pan, pour the milk mixture into it and cook over a gentle heat, stirring with a wooden spoon until the custard thickens enough to coat the back of the spoon. Once it has thickened, remove from the heat, transfer the custard to a clean bowl, cover and leave to cool.

When cold, use a whisk to stir in 300ml/½ pint/1¼ cups double (heavy) cream. Chill until ready to use.

Variations

Replace the bara brith with other teabread or cake, such as the boiled fruit cake on page 90. In place of brandy or whisky try using a Welsh liqueur such as Black Mountain, made with blackcurrants and apples.

Per portion Energy 340kcal/1415kJ; Protein 4.5g; Carbohydrate 25.6g, of which sugars 13.1g; Fat 22.8g, of which saturates 13.1g; Cholesterol 53mg; Calcium 106mg; Fibre 0.7g; Sodium 123mg

Fruit turnovers

Before ovens were introduced, the Welsh housewife would cook turnovers and even large fruit tarts on the bakestone – and what a skilled job it must have been to get the temperature just right and to flip them over without losing the filling. This recipe for *Teisennau frwythau ar y maen* uses plums, but you could use apples, rhubarb or a jar of ready-made fruit compote. Butter gives the pastry a good flavour while the lard makes it crisp.

2 Sift the flour and salt into a bowl, add the lard or cooking fat and butter and rub them into the flour until the mixture resembles fine crumbs (alternatively, process in a food processor). Stir in enough cold water until the mixture forms clumps, then gather together to make a smooth dough. Wrap the pastry and chill for 20–30 minutes to allow it to relax.

3 Preheat the oven to 190°C/375°F/ Gas 5. Then line a baking sheet with baking parchment.

4 On a lightly floured surface, roll out the dough to 3–5mm/⅛–¼in thick. Using a small upturned bowl or plate as a guide, cut out eight 15cm/6in circles, re-rolling the pastry offcuts as necessary.

5 Place a spoonful of cooled fruit on to each pastry circle and brush the edges with water. Fold the pastry over the fruit, pinching the edges to seal them well. Arrange the pastries on the baking sheet, brush with milk, sprinkle some sugar over and make a small slit in each.

6 Put into the hot oven and cook for 20–30 minutes until golden brown. Sprinkle with a little extra sugar and transfer to a wire rack to cool.

Makes 8

450g/1lb plums, stones (pits) removed and chopped

25–40g/1–1½oz/2–3 tbsp sugar

350g/12oz/3 cups plain (all-purpose) flour

85g/3oz/6 tbsp lard or white cooking fat, cut into pieces

85g/3oz/6 tbsp butter, cut into pieces

milk and sugar for brushing and sprinkling

pinch of salt

1 Bring the fruit and the sugar to the boil with 15ml/1tbsp water, then cover and simmer for 5–10 minutes, stirring frequently, until the fruit is soft. You can reduce the liquid by bubbling uncovered and stirring until thick. Leave to cool.

Per portion Energy 340kcal/1420kJ; Protein 4.2g; Carbohydrate 38.5g, of which sugars 5.1g; Fat 19.8g, of which saturates 9.9g; Cholesterol 33mg; Calcium 66mg; Fibre 1.5g; Sodium 66mg

Spiced plums with flummery topping

The English word flummery stems from *Llymru*, which is Welsh for the early method of cooking oats in water to make a jelly-like dish. The recipe has since developed, first with the addition of milk and later to become a dish of whipped cream and toasted oats. This version of *Eirin sbeislyd gyda chaenen lymru* is laced with Welsh whisky, though it would also be good with mead or one of the new breed of Welsh liqueurs.

Serves 4

8–12 plums

2.5ml/½ tsp mixed (apple pie) spice

25g/1oz/2 tbsp sugar, or to taste

30g/1oz/4 tbsp medium oatmeal

300ml/½ pint/1¼ cups double (heavy) cream

30ml/2 tbsp clear honey

30ml/2 tbsp Welsh whisky

1 Quarter the plums and remove their stones (pits). Put the fruit in a pan with 60ml/4 tbsp water and the mixed spice. Bring just to the boil, cover and cook gently until the plums are soft, stirring occasionally and adding a little extra water if necessary to keep them moist (cooking time will depend on the ripeness of the fruit). Remove from the heat and stir in the sugar to taste. Leave to cool.

2 Heat a frying pan, add the oatmeal and toss or stir it until golden brown. Tip on to a plate and leave to cool.

Variation
In place of plums, try fresh ripe berries or apricot slices sprinkled with brown sugar, or soft-cooked apples or pears.

3 Whip the cream until thick but not stiff. Blend the honey with the whisky and add to the cream. Continue whipping until the cream thickens again and soft peaks form. Stir in three-quarters of the toasted oatmeal (take care not to over mix).

4 Spoon the plums and their juices into the bottom of the serving glasses and then top each one with a layer of the cream and oatmeal mixture. Sprinkle the remaining toasted oatmeal over the top and chill the glasses in the refrigerator.

Per portion Energy 540kcal/2243kJ; Protein 3.8g; Carbohydrate 35.5g, of which sugars 24.5g; Fat 41.7g, of which saturates 25.1g; Cholesterol 103mg; Calcium 64mg; Fibre 2.8g; Sodium 25mg

Breads, cakes & pancakes

Baking day and tea-time have long been traditions in Wales, with mountains of bread and spiced cakes to take the family through the week. Nowhere has the bakestone been more utilized than in the Welsh kitchen – to make pancakes, griddle cakes and bread. There are cakes that can be rustled up for unexpected guests and cakes that will keep for several days, ready to fill out the lunch boxes of hard-working hill farmers, miners, quarry workers and fishermen.

Traditional bara brith

Bara Brith means "speckled bread" and that's just what this is – spicy yeasted bread speckled with dried fruit that has been plumped up in tea. Early types were likely to have been made from dough left over from bread making, with every family having its own favourite version. Serve it sliced thickly and spread with salty Welsh butter.

Makes 1 large loaf

225g/8oz/1⅓ cups mixed dried fruit and chopped mixed (candied) peel

350ml/12fl oz/1½ cups hot strong tea, strained

450g/1lb/4 cups strong white bread flour

50g/2oz/4 tbsp soft brown sugar

5ml/1 tsp salt

2.5ml/½ tsp mixed (apple pie) spice

30ml/2¼ tsp easy-blend (rapid-mix) yeast

50g/2oz/¼ cup butter, melted

milk, to mix

1 Put the fruit into a heatproof bowl and pour the hot tea over it. Cover and leave to stand at room temperature for several hours or overnight.

2 Sift the flour, sugar, salt and mixed spice into a large warmed mixing bowl. Stir in the yeast.

3 Add the fruit and its liquid and the melted butter. Stir well until the mixture can be gathered together to make a ball of soft smooth dough, adding a little milk if necessary. With your hands and on a lightly floured surface, mix and stretch the dough until it becomes smooth, firm and elastic. Return the dough to the cleaned bowl. Cover with oiled cling film (plastic wrap) and leave in a warm place for about 1½ hours, or until the dough has more or less doubled its size.

4 Grease a 900g/2lb loaf tin (pan) and line it with baking parchment.

5 Turn the risen dough on to a lightly floured surface, gently press the air out, and then shape it into a loaf. Put it, seam-side down, into the prepared tin. Cover with oiled clear film (plastic wrap) and leave in a warm place for about 1–1½ hours until the loaf has again just about doubled in size.

6 Preheat the oven to 200°C/400°F/ Gas 6. Put into the hot oven and cook for about 40 minutes until well risen, golden brown and cooked through. To test, turn the loaf out of its tin and tap the underneath – it should sound hollow.

7 Turn out and cool on a wire rack.

Per loaf Energy 2730kcal/11567kJ; Protein 49.7g; Carbohydrate 557.8g, of which sugars 214.9g; Fat 48.7g, of which saturates 27.5g; Cholesterol 110mg; Calcium 890mg; Fibre 18.9g; Sodium 2414mg

Bara brith teabread

This spiced loaf has become widely known as *Bara Brith*, though the method of making it is nothing like the original yeasted bread. Once the fruit has been plumped up by soaking it in tea, this version is quick to make with self-raising flour. It is meant to be sliced and buttered though, to my mind, it tastes good just as it is.

Makes 1 large loaf

225g/8oz/1⅓ cups mixed dried fruit and chopped mixed (candied) peel

225ml/8fl oz/1 cup hot strong tea, strained

225g/8oz/2 cups self-raising (self-rising) flour

5ml/1 tsp mixed (apple pie) spice

25g/1oz/2 tbsp butter

100g/3¾oz/8 tbsp soft brown sugar

1 egg, lightly beaten

1 Put the fruit into a heatproof bowl and pour the hot tea over it. Cover and leave to stand at room temperature for

2 Preheat the oven to 180°C/350°F/ Gas 4. Grease a 900g/2lb loaf tin (pan) and line it with baking parchment.

3 Sift the flour and the mixed spice into a large mixing bowl. Add the butter and, with your fingertips, rub it into the flour until the mixture starts to resemble fine breadcrumbs.

4 Stir in the sugar, then add the fruit and its liquid along with the beaten egg. Stir well to make a mixture with a soft consistency.

5 Transfer the mixture to the prepared loaf tin and level the surface.

6 Put into the hot oven and cook for about 1 hour or until a skewer inserted in the centre comes out clean.

7 Turn out on a wire rack and leave to cool completely.

Cook's tip
The flavour of the loaf can be varied subtly by using a variety of teas – try the distinctive perfume of Earl Grey.

Per loaf Energy 2024kcal/8588kJ; Protein 33.2g; Carbohydrate 432.7g, of which sugars 261.3g; Fat 29.9g, of which saturates 15g; Cholesterol 244mg; Calcium 565mg; Fibre 11.9g; Sodium 342mg

Welsh cakes

Their Welsh name, *Pice ar y maen*, translates into "cakes on the stone". These speckled discs were cooked at least once a week in kitchens throughout Wales, to cheer up a cup of tea or offer a traditional welcome to visitors. Originally cooked on a bakestone over the fire or in a Dutch oven, they have long been cooked straight on the solid plates of ranges, an Aga or Rayburn, but are now made on a bakestone. Many cooks use half lard and half butter. Serve the Welsh cakes warm or cold, as they are, or buttered.

3 Lightly beat the egg and with a round-end knife and a cutting action stir it into the flour mixture with enough milk to gather the mixture into a ball of soft dough.

4 Transfer to a lightly floured surface and roll out to about 5mm/¼in thick. With a 6–7.5cm/ 2½ –3in cutter, cut out rounds, gathering up the offcuts and re-rolling to make more.

5 Smear a little butter or oil over the hot bakestone or pan and cook the cakes, in small batches, for about 4–5 minutes on each side or until they are slightly risen, golden brown and cooked through.

6 Transfer to a wire rack, dust with caster sugar on both sides and leave to cool.

Makes about 16

250g/9oz/2 cups plain (all-purpose) flour

7.5ml/1¼ tsp baking powder

125g/4½oz/½ cup butter, cut into small cubes

100g/3½oz/½ cup caster (superfine) sugar

75g/3oz/½ cup currants

1 egg

45ml/3 tbsp milk

caster sugar, for dusting

1 Heat the bakestone or a heavy frying pan over medium to low heat.

2 Sift the flour, baking powder and salt into a large mixing bowl. Then add the butter and, with your fingertips, rub it into the flour until the mixture resembles fine breadcrumbs. Alternatively, you can process the ingredients in a food processor. Stir in the sugar and currants.

Variation
For a change, add a large pinch of mixed spice to the flour in step 2, or a little vanilla extract to the egg in step 3.

Per portion Energy 128kcal/540kJ; Protein 4.1g; Carbohydrate 22.8g, of which sugars 1.3g; Fat 2.9g, of which saturates 1.4g; Cholesterol 29mg; Calcium 66mg; Fibre 0.9g; Sodium 29mg

Bakestone bread

A loaf of bread that is cooked on the hob – watch it rise and marvel! The finished *Bara pl.anc* has a distinctive appearance with a soft texture and scorched crust. If you have a bread machine, do use it on a short programme to make the dough and then continue with steps 3–7. Make sure to use ordinary plain flour and not strong bread flour.

Makes 1 loaf

500g/1lb 2oz/4¼ cups plain (all-purpose) flour

5ml/1 tsp fine sea salt

5ml/1 tsp sugar

7.5ml/1½ tsp easy-blend (rapid-rise) yeast

150ml/1¼ pint milk

15g/½oz/1 tbsp butter, cut into small pieces

5ml/1 tsp oil

1 Put the flour into a large bowl and add the salt, sugar and yeast. Combine the milk with 150ml/¼ pint/⅔ cup water and add the butter. Heat gently until the liquid is lukewarm when tested with your little finger. Stir the liquid into the flour to make a ragged mixture then, gather it together to make a dough ball.

2 Tip the dough on to a lightly floured surface and knead it until smooth, firm and elastic. Then put the oil in a large bowl and turn the dough in it until it is lightly coated. Cover the dough with cling film (plastic wrap) or a damp tea towel and leave to rise for about 1½ hours, or until just about doubled in size.

3 Tip the dough out on to a lightly floured surface and knead (gently this time) just until the dough becomes smooth – it will be soft and stretchy. On the same floured surface and using your hands or a rolling pin, press the dough into a rough circle measuring about 20cm/8in in diameter and 2cm/¾in thick. Leave to stand for 15 minutes to allow the dough to relax.

4 Meanwhile, heat a bakestone or heavy frying pan over a medium heat.

5 Using a wide spatula and your hands, lift the dough on to the warm surface and leave it to cook gently for 20 minutes.

6 Turn the bread over – it may sink, but will soon start rising again. Gently cook the second side for about 20 minutes. The top and bottom crusts should be firm and browned while the sides remain pale. When the sides are pressed with the fingers, they should feel softly firm.

7 Leave to cool on a wire rack.

Per loaf Energy 1928kcal/8179kJ; Protein 52.2g; Carbohydrate 399.8g, of which sugars 18.8g; Fat 24.4g, of which saturates 10.8g; Cholesterol 41mg; Calcium 885mg; Fibre 15.5g; Sodium 2136mg

Welsh crumpets

These yeast pancakes or *Crempogau burum* can be served hot and buttered, or with sweet or savoury accompaniments. Try them for breakfast, American style, with crispy bacon and a thin drizzle of clear honey or maple syrup. Cook them in buttered metal rings or make them freeform. The best results come from using strong bread flour, though ordinary plain flour works well too.

Makes 8–10

225g/8oz/2 cups strong (bread) or plain (all-purpose) flour

2.5ml/½ tsp fine sea salt

6.25ml/1¼ tsp quick or easy-bake yeast

150ml/¼ pint/⅔ cup milk

15g/½oz/1 tbsp butter

1 egg

Melted butter, for brushing

1 Sift the flour and salt into a large jug (pitcher) or bowl and stir in the yeast. Combine the milk with 150ml/¼ pint/⅔ cup water and add the butter. Warm gently (on the hob or in the microwave) until the liquid is lukewarm when tested with your little finger. With a whisk, beat in the egg. Still with the whisk, stir the liquid into the flour to make a thick smooth batter. Cover and leave to stand at room temperature for about 1 hour to allow the yeast to start working.

2 Preheat a bakestone or heavy frying pan over medium to medium-low heat.

3 Brush melted butter on the inside of three or four metal rings (each measuring about 9cm/3½in) and lightly butter the hot bakestone or pan.

4 Place the metal rings on the hot surface. Pour a generous spoonful of batter into each one. Alternatively, drop generous spoonfuls of batter on to the hot buttered surface to make pancakes about 9cm/3½in in diameter, allowing some space between each one for the spreading of the batter.

5 Cook for a minute or two until the underside is golden brown, bubbles have burst on the surface and the top is just set. Carefully remove the metal rings and with a spatula, gently turn the crumpets over. Cook the second side until light golden brown. Lift off and keep warm.

6 Repeat with the remaining batter.

Cook's tip
Sprinkle the warm pancakes with sugar, into which you have mixed some ground cinnamon.

Per portion Energy 102kcal/432kJ; Protein 3.3g; Carbohydrate 18.2g, of which sugars 1.1g; Fat 2.3g, of which saturates 1.1g; Cholesterol 23mg; Calcium 53mg; Fibre 0.7g; Sodium 23mg

Pancakes

Crempogau are the pancakes you will see on traditional baking stalls at markets such as Swansea. They are simple to make. Either sprinkle a few currants in the centre as they cook or leave them plain. Years ago, they would have been served spread with salty Welsh butter and sugar, piled high and cut into wedges like a cake. They are also lovely served sprinkled with a little lemon juice and sugar, or drizzled with honey or golden syrup.

Makes 12–14

about 150ml/¼ pint/⅔ cup milk

225g/8oz/2 cups plain (all-purpose) flour

2 eggs

25g/1oz/2 tbsp butter, plus extra for greasing

currants

1 Top up the milk with water to make 300ml/½ pint/1¼ cups. Sift the flour into a large bowl or jug (pitcher). Make a well in the centre and break the eggs into it. With a whisk, stir in the eggs, gradually adding the milk mixture to make a smooth pouring batter.

2 Melt the butter and stir in with the whisk. Leave the batter to stand for 30 minutes and stir well before using.

3 Preheat a bakestone or heavy frying pan over medium heat.

4 Lightly butter the hot surface and add a large spoonful of batter to make a pancake about 15-20cm/6-8in across. Cook for a minute or so until the underside is golden brown. Just as the top is about to set, scatter a few currants in the centre (so that they stick but do not sink completely into the batter).

5 With a wide spatula, carefully flip the pancake over and briefly cook the second side until golden brown and set. Lift off and keep warm.

6 Repeat with the remaining batter.

Cook's tip
This batter can be used to make thin, lacy pancakes by thinning it with a little extra milk, so the mixture spreads on the hot surface.

Per portion Energy 84kcal/352kJ; Protein 2.8g; Carbohydrate 13g, of which sugars 0.8g; Fat 2.7g, of which saturates 1.3g; Cholesterol 32mg; Calcium 40mg; Fibre 0.5g; Sodium 26mg

Shearing cake

To this day sheep shearing provides a good excuse for a rural get-together. The tradition was always to serve the buttery seed cake, *Cacen gneifio,* as part of the shearers' well-earned refreshment. A similar cake would also be made during harvesting. It, too, contained caraway seeds and was aptly named threshing cake.

Makes a 20cm/8in cake

225g/8oz/2 cups plain (all-purpose) flour

5ml/1 tsp baking powder

175g/6oz/¾ cup butter, softened

175g/6oz/¾ cup caster (superfine) sugar

3 eggs, beaten

50g/2oz/⅓ cup finely chopped mixed (candied) peel

10ml/2 tsp caraway seeds

1 Preheat the oven to 180°C/350°F/ Gas 4. Lightly butter a 20cm/8 in round cake tin and line it with baking parchment. Sift the flour with the baking powder.

2 Beat the butter and sugar in a bowl until light and fluffy. Beat in the eggs, a little at a time. Using a metal spoon, fold in the flour mixture, mixed peel, caraway seeds and milk to make a soft mix.

3 Spoon the mixture into the prepared tin and level the surface. Put into the hot oven and cook for 1–1¼ hours or until firm to the touch and cooked through – a skewer inserted in the centre should come out clean.

4 Cool for 15 minutes, then turn out on to a wire rack and leave to cool completely.

Per cake Energy 3109kcal/13026kJ; Protein 43g; Carbohydrate 389.7g, of which sugars 218.3g; Fat 164.4g, of which saturates 96.6g; Cholesterol 946mg; Calcium 626mg; Fibre 9.4g; Sodium 1441mg

Light cakes

These pancakes or *Leicecs* are sweet with sugar and should be kept small (otherwise they are difficult to turn). They need a well buttered or oiled surface for cooking. Aim for pancakes with one side that is smooth and golden brown with the other lacy, full of holes and lightly browned. Eat them warm off the bakestone with butter, maybe with fresh soft fruit such as raspberries.

Makes 12–14

125g/4½oz/1 cup plain (all-purpose) flour

1.25ml/¼ tsp bicarbonate of soda

pinch of salt

75g/3oz/⅔ cup caster (superfine) sugar

1 egg

about 90ml/6 tbsp buttermilk or milk

1 Preheat the bakestone or heavy-base frying pan over medium heat.

2 Sift the flour, bicarbonate of soda and salt into a bowl and stir in the sugar.

3 With a whisk beat the egg into the flour, and then add enough milk to make a batter.

4 Butter the hot bakestone. Drop spoonfuls of batter on the surface to make pancakes about 7.5–10cm/3–4in in diameter, allowing space between.

5 Cook for a minute or two until the underside is golden brown and small bubbles have risen to the top surface and burst open. With a metal spatula, carefully flip the pancakes over and briefly cook the second side until light golden brown and set. Lift off and keep warm on a warm dish.

6 Repeat with the remaining pancake batter to make 12–14 pancakes. They are best served warm and certainly should be eaten on the day they are made.

Per portion Energy 60kcal/254kJ; Protein 1.5g; Carbohydrate 12.8g, of which sugars 6g; Fat 0.6g, of which saturates 0.2g; Cholesterol 14mg; Calcium 25mg; Fibre 0.3g; Sodium 8mg

Anglesey shortbread

Originating in Aberffraw, a village on Anglesey, these biscuits, called *Teisen Berffro,* were decorated with a shell motif depicting the sign of pilgrims on their way to the church at Santiago de Compostela in northern Spain. They are made by pressing the dough into a queen scallop shell prior to baking. They do, of course, taste just as good without the marking.

3 Work the dough so that the warmth of your hand keeps the dough soft and pliable. Divide and shape it into 12 balls.

4 Sprinkle the inside of a scallop shell with sugar, gently press a ball of dough into it, spreading it evenly so the shell is filled. Invert on to the paper-lined sheet, pressing it down to flatten the base and to mark it with the impression of the shell. Lift the shell off, carefully prising out the dough. Alternatively, press or roll the dough balls into plain biscuits (cookies) measuring about 5cm/2in across.

5 Put into the hot oven and cook for about 10 minutes until set. Traditionally, they should not be allowed to brown, but they look very attractive and taste delicious with crisp golden edges.

6 Sprinkle with a little extra sugar, transfer to a wire rack and leave to cool completely.

Cook's tip
Although shaping the first shell-shape biscuit may seen tricky, the shell will coat with sugar and the rest will slip out easily. You could flavour the mixture with vanilla or spices in step 2.

Makes 12

100g/3½oz/½ cup butter, softened

50g/2oz/¼ cup caster (superfine) sugar, plus extra for sprinkling

150g/5½oz/1¼ cups plain (all-purpose) flour

1 Preheat the oven to 200°C/400°F/ Gas 6. Then line a baking sheet with baking parchment.

2 Put the butter and sugar into a bowl and beat until light and fluffy. Sift the flour over and stir it in until the mixture can be gathered into a ball of soft dough.

Per portion Energy 121kcal/506kJ; Protein 1.2g; Carbohydrate 14.1g, of which sugars 4.6g; Fat 7g, of which saturates 4.4g; Cholesterol 18mg; Calcium 21mg; Fibre 0.4g; Sodium 51mg

Old-fashioned treacle cake

Like the other quick-to-make cake, *Teisen Lap* on page 94, *Teisen driog hen ffasiwn* would have been baked on an enamel plate. The treacle gives it a rich colour and a deep flavour and the sight of it must have been most welcome to miners and other workers when they opened their "box" during their well-earned meal break.

Makes a 20cm/8in cake

250g/9oz/2 cups self-raising (self-rising) flour

2.5ml/½ tsp mixed (apple pie) spice

75g/3oz/6 tbsp butter, cut into small cubes

35g/1oz/2 tbsp caster (superfine) sugar

150g/5oz/1 cup mixed dried fruit

1 egg

15ml/1 tbsp black treacle (molasses)

100ml/3½fl oz/scant ½ cup milk

3 Beat the egg and, with a small whisk or a fork, stir in the treacle and then the milk. Stir the liquid into the flour to make a fairly stiff but moist consistency adding a little extra milk if necessary.

4 Transfer the cake mixture to the prepared dish or tin with a spoon and level out the surface.

5 Bake the cake in the hot oven and cook for about 1 hour until it has risen, is firm to the touch and fully cooked through. To check if the cake is cooked, insert a small skewer in the centre – it should come out free of sticky mixture.

6 Leave the cooked treacle cake to cool completely. Serve it, cut into wedges, straight from the dish.

1 Preheat the oven to 180°C/350°F/Gas 5. Butter a shallow 20–23cm/8–9in ovenproof flan dish or baking tin (pan).

2 Sift the flour and spice into a large mixing bowl. Add the butter and, with your fingertips, rub it into the flour until the mixture resembles fine crumbs. Alternatively you could do this in a food processor. Stir in the sugar and mixed dried fruit.

Cook's tip
Vary the fruit – try using chopped ready-to-eat dried apricots and stem ginger, or a packet of luxury dried fruit.

Per cake Energy 2089kcal/8805kJ; Protein 37.4g; Carbohydrate 343g, of which sugars 152.4g; Fat 72.8g, of which saturates 42.2g; Cholesterol 356mg; Calcium 720mg; Fibre 11.1g; Sodium 676mg

Boiled fruit cake

The texture of *Teisen ffrwythau wedi ei berwi* is quite distinctive – moist and plump as a result of boiling the dried fruit with the butter, sugar and milk prior to baking. For special occasions replace some of the milk with sherry or brandy and arrange cherries and nuts on the surface of the uncooked cake before putting it in the oven. It makes an ideal Christmas cake, too.

Makes a 20cm/8in cake

350g/12oz/2 cups mixed dried fruit

225g/8oz/1 cup butter

225g/8oz/1 cup soft dark brown sugar

400ml/14fl oz/1⅔ cup milk

450g/1lb/4 cups self-raising (self-rising) flour

5ml/1 tsp bicarbonate of soda (baking soda)

5ml/1 tsp mixed (apple pie) spice

2 eggs, beaten

1 Preheat the oven to 160°C/325°F/ Gas 3. Lightly grease a 20cm/8in round cake tin (pan) and line it with baking parchment.

2 Put the dried fruit in a large pan and add the butter and sugar. Bring slowly to boil, stirring occasionally. When the butter has melted and the sugar has dissolved, bubble the mixture gently for about 2 minutes. Remove from the heat and cool slightly.

3 Sift the flour with the bicarbonate of soda and mixed spice. Add this and the eggs to the fruit mixture and mix together well.

4 Pour the mixture into the prepared tin and smooth the surface.

5 Bake for about 1½ hours or until firm to the touch and the cake is cooked through – a skewer inserted in the centre should come out free of sticky mixture.

6 Leave in the tin to cool for 20–30 minutes, then turn out and cool completely on a wire rack.

Per cake Energy 5150kcal/21689kJ; Protein 72.2g; Carbohydrate 796g, of which sugars 498.8g; Fat 209.1g, of which saturates 125.4g; Cholesterol 884mg; Calcium 2352mg; Fibre 20.1g; Sodium 3297mg

Overnight cake

Many old recipes for cakes contained lists of ingredients with weights and proportions that were easy to remember – ideal for passing down the line from generation to generation. This one, *Teisen dros nos*, has no added sugar and is at its most delicious eaten cooled on the day it is made, its crust being crisp and flaky while the inside is soft and moist.

Makes a thin 23cm/9in cake

225g/8oz/2 cups plain (all-purpose) flour

5ml/1 tsp ground cinnamon

5ml/1 tsp ground ginger

115g/4oz/½ cup butter, cut into cubes

115g/4oz/⅔ cup mixed dried fruit

2.5ml/½ tsp bicarbonate of soda (baking soda)

15ml/1 tbsp vinegar

300ml/½ pint/1¼ cups milk

3 Preheat the oven to 180°C/360°F/Gas 4. Grease a shallow 23cm/9 in round cake tin (pan) and line its base with baking parchment. Spoon the cake mixture into the prepared tin and level the top.

4 Put into the hot oven and cook for about 1 hour or until firm to the touch and cooked through – a skewer inserted in the centre should come out free of sticky mixture. If the top starts to get too brown during cooking, cover it with baking parchment.

5 Leave in the tin to cool for 15–20 minutes, then turn out and cool completely on a wire rack.

Cook's tip
The low sugar content of this cake makes it ideal for serving with thin slices of crumbly cheese such as Caerphilly.

1 Sift the flour and spices. Add the butter and rub in until the mixture resembles fine breadcrumbs. Stir in the dried fruit and enough milk to make a soft mix.

2 Mix the bicarbonate of soda with the vinegar and, as it froths, quickly stir it into the mixture. Cover the bowl and leave at room temperature for about 8 hours.

Per cake Energy 2069kcal/8681kJ; Protein 34.7g; Carbohydrate 267.9g, of which sugars 96.5g; Fat 103g, of which saturates 63.6g; Cholesterol 263mg; Calcium 780mg; Fibre 9.5g; Sodium 888mg

Honey and spice cakes

The Welsh have always enjoyed using spices and indeed they still do. These golden little cakes, *Teisenni mêl a sbeis*, are fragrant with honey and cinnamon. Though their appearance is more traditional when cooked directly in a bun tin, they tend to rise higher (and are therefore lighter) when baked in paper cases.

3 Beat the butter with the sugar until light and fluffy. Beat in the egg yolk, then gradually add the honey.

4 With a large metal spoon and a cutting action, fold in the flour mixture plus sufficient milk to make a soft mixture that will just drop off the spoon.

5 In a separate bowl whisk the egg white until stiff peaks form. Using a large metal spoon, fold the egg white into the cake mixture.

Makes 18

250g/9oz/2 cups plain (all-purpose) flour

5ml/1 tsp ground cinnamon

5ml/1 tsp bicarbonate of soda (baking soda)

125g/4½oz/½ cup butter, softened

125g/4½oz/10 tbsp soft brown sugar

1 large (US extra large) egg, separated

125g/4½oz clear honey

about 60ml/4 tbsp milk

caster (superfine) sugar for sprinkling

1 Preheat the oven to 200°C/400°F/ Gas 6. Butter the holes of a bun tin (pan) or, alternatively, line them with paper cases.

2 Sift the flour into a large mixing bowl with the cinnamon and the bicarbonate of soda.

6 Divide the mixture among the paper cases or the holes in the prepared tin. Put into the hot oven and cook for 15–20 minutes or until risen, firm to the touch and golden brown.

7 Sprinkle the tops lightly with caster sugar and leave to cool completely on a wire rack.

Per portion Energy 152kcal/639kJ; Protein 1.9g; Carbohydrate 23.6g, of which sugars 13g; Fat 6.3g, of which saturates 3.8g; Cholesterol 26mg; Calcium 30mg; Fibre 0.4g; Sodium 49mg

Tinker's cakes

These delicate little cakes, *Teisenni tincar*, could be rustled up in next to no time for eating hot off the bakestone when visitors or the travelling pot mender or tinker, called. The quantities have been kept small because they really must be eaten while still really fresh. To make more, simply double up on the measures.

Makes 8–10

125g/4½oz/1 cup self-raising (self-rising) flour

small pinch of salt

70g/2½oz/5 tbsp butter, cut into small cubes

50g/2oz/4 tbsp demerara (raw) or light muscovado (brown) sugar

1 small cooking apple, weighing about 150g/5oz

about 30ml/2 tbsp milk

caster (superfine) sugar, for dusting

1 Preheat the bakestone or heavy frying pan over low to medium heat.

2 Sift the flour and salt into a mixing bowl. Add the butter and, with your fingertips, rub it into the flour until the mixture resembles fine breadcrumbs. Alternatively, whiz the ingredients in a food processor. Stir in the sugar.

3 Peel and grate the apple, discarding the core, and stir the grated apple into the flour mixture with enough milk to make a mixture than can be gathered into a ball of soft, moist dough. Work it slightly to make sure the flour is mixed in well.

4 Transfer to a lightly floured surface and roll out the dough to about 5mm/¼in thick. With a 6–7.5cm/ 2½–3in cutter, cut out rounds, gathering up the offcuts and re-rolling them to make more.

5 Smear a little butter on the hot bakestone or pan and cook the cakes, in batches, for about 4–5 minutes on each side or until golden brown and cooked through.

6 Lift on to a wire rack and dust with caster sugar. Serve warm.

Cook's tip
Add a good pinch of ground cinnamon or mixed spice to the flour. The rolled-out dough could just as easily be cut into squares or triangles for a change.

Per portion Energy 121kcal/508kJ; Protein 1.4g; Carbohydrate 16.5g, of which sugars 6.9g; Fat 6g, of which saturates 3.7g; Cholesterol 15mg; Calcium 26mg; Fibre 0.6g; Sodium 45mg

Teisen lap

A moist cake (*lap* means moist) with a crisp crust, *Teisen lap* was popular with coal miners in South Wales, as it made ideal fare for their lunch boxes. Originally it would have been cooked in a Dutch oven in front of the open fire, either in the oblong tray that came with the oven or on an enamel plate. Here, it is baked in a shallow tin in the oven and can be served warm or cold.

Makes a 20–23cm/8–9in cake

250g/9oz/2 cups plain (all-purpose) flour

7.5ml/1½ tsp baking powder

pinch of salt

2.5ml/½ tsp grated nutmeg

125g/4½oz/9 tbsp butter, cut into small cubes

125g/4½oz/½ cup caster (superfine) sugar

125g/4½oz/½ cup currants or sultanas (golden raisins)

2 eggs, lightly beaten

150ml/¼ pint/⅔ cup milk or buttermilk

1 Preheat the oven to 190°C/375°F/ Gas 5. Butter a shallow 20–23cm/8–9in round baking tin (pan).

2 Sift the flour, baking powder, salt and nutmeg into a large mixing bowl and stir in the sugar. Add the butter and, with your fingertips, rub it into the flour until the mixture resembles fine crumbs. Alternatively, do this in a food processor. Stir in the currants. Stir in the eggs with enough milk to give a mixture with a soft consistency that easily drops off the spoon.

3 Transfer the mixture to the prepared cake tin and level the surface.

4 Bake in the hot oven for 30–40 minutes, or until the cake has risen, is golden brown and cooked through. To check, a small skewer inserted in the centre should come out clean.

5 Leave in the tin for 5 minutes then turn out and cool on a wire rack.

Cook's tip
Replace the currants or sultanas with chopped ready-to-eat dried apricots.

Per cake Energy 2831kcal/11903kJ; Protein 45.1g; Carbohydrate 419.3g, of which sugars 228.8g; Fat 120.1g, of which saturates 70.3g; Cholesterol 656mg; Calcium 733mg; Fibre 10.3g; Sodium 1052mg

Index

Bibliography

A Welsh Welcome, Wales Gas Board 1957
Davies, Gilli, *Lamb, Leeks & Laverbread*, Grafton 1989
Freeman, Bobby, *An Examination of Welsh cookery traditions and
    their curious denial by the Welsh*, Oxford Food Symposium 1981
Freeman, Bobby, *First Catch Your Peacock*, Y Llolfa 1996
Llanover, The Right Hon. Lady, *The First Principles of Good
    Cookery*, Brefi Press 1991
Owen, Trevor M., *Customs and Traditions of Wales*, University of
    Wales Press and The Western Mail 1991
Pressdee, Colin, *Food Wales*, Graffeg 2005
Tibbott, S. Minwel, *Baking in Wales*, National Museum of Wales,
    1991
Tibbott, S. Minwel, *Cooking on the Open Hearth*, National
    Museum of Wales, 1982
Tibbott, S. Minwel, *Domestic Life in Wales*, National Museums &
    Galleries of Wales, 2002
Tibbott, S. Minwel, *Welsh Fare*, National Museum of Wales, 1976
Tibbott, S. Minwel and Thomas, Beth, *A Woman's Work*, National
    Museum of Wales, 1994

Acknowledgements

Author's acknowledgements

The author would like to thank the following people and
organizations for their help in writing this book: Mared Wyn
McAleavey, Curator of Domestic Life at The Museum of Welsh
Life in St. Fagans, whose friendly assistance and encouragement
were so appreciated; Sue James, a good friend, for her help and
generosity in providing Welsh translations of the recipe titles; and
the following websites: www.bbc.co.uk/wales,
www.foodwales.com, and www.welshblackcattlesociety.org.

Publisher's acknowledgements

The publisher would like to thank the following for the use of
their pictures in the book (l=left, r=right, t=top, b=bottom,
m=middle): p7b, p8b, p11b National Museums and Galleries of
Wales; p6, p8t, p9t, p9b, p10, p11t, p12t Alamy.
All other photographs © Anness Publishing Ltd.